THE LEADERSHIP BLUEPRINT

A Guide to Brilliance for Teens and Young Adults

Dileep Kumar

Chennai • Bangalore

CLEVER FOX PUBLISHING
Chennai, India

Published by CLEVER FOX PUBLISHING 2023
Copyright © Dileep Kumar 2023

All Rights Reserved.
Hardback ISBN: 978-93-56484-81-8
Paperback ISBN: 978-93-56484-39-9

This book has been published with all reasonable efforts taken to make the material error-free after the consent of the author. No part of this book shall be used, reproduced in any manner whatsoever without written permission from the author, except in the case of brief quotations embodied in critical articles and reviews.

The Author of this book is solely responsible and liable for its content including but not limited to the views, representations, descriptions, statements, information, opinions and references ["Content"]. The Content of this book shall not constitute or be construed or deemed to reflect the opinion or expression of the Publisher or Editor. Neither the Publisher nor Editor endorse or approve the Content of this book or guarantee the reliability, accuracy or completeness of the Content published herein and do not make any representations or warranties of any kind, express or implied, including but not limited to the implied warranties of merchantability, fitness for a particular purpose. The Publisher and Editor shall not be liable whatsoever for any errors, omissions, whether such errors or omissions result from negligence, accident, or any other cause or claims for loss or damages of any kind, including without limitation, indirect or consequential loss or damage arising out of use, inability to use, or about the reliability, accuracy or sufficiency of the information contained in this book.

Disclaimer

Although efforts have been made to ensure accuracy, the author and publisher do not assume liability for any losses incurred by individuals who rely solely on the information. The content is intended for general informational and educational purposes.

Dedication

To those who taught me, guided me, and inspired me throughout my journey.

To my mentors and role models whose wisdom and guidance have shaped my path.

To my family whose constant support and love have been my foundation.

To the young minds—the budding leaders of today and the visionaries of tomorrow. May your journey be filled with empowerment, growth, and the realization of your brilliance.

ACKNOWLEDGEMENTS

*H*olding this book in my hands reminds me of many individuals who have played a significant role in its creation. Their steadfast support, guidance, and belief have transformed my vision into reality.

First and foremost, I extend my deepest gratitude to the divine force that guides us all. Your presence has been a strength throughout this journey, offering me the courage to pursue this endeavour with determination and purpose.

To my mentors and teachers, who have been my guiding lights. Your wisdom, encouragement, and willingness to share your knowledge have shaped my understanding of leadership and its transformative power. Your influence continues to resonate in every word of this book.

My family, whose love and unwavering support have been my solid foundation. Your belief in my abilities, even during moments of self-doubt, has reminded me that it's crucial to challenge myself and aim for greatness by pushing my limits.

To my friends and colleagues, your camaraderie and encouragement have infused joy into this journey. Your shared experiences and insightful discussions have enriched the content of this book and remind me of the incredible power of collaboration.

I want to express my heartfelt thanks to all those who have been involved in getting my work published.

To those who believed in the potential of this project, your encouragement and enthusiasm kept me motivated during the writing process. Your feedback, suggestions, and critiques have been invaluable in refining the ideas presented in these pages.

Lastly, to you, the reader. Whether you're a teenager seeking empowerment, a young adult navigating uncharted waters, or anyone seeking to understand the essence of leadership, this book is a product of the collective effort and dedication of those who believe in the transformative potential of every individual.

CONTENTS

Preface vi

Introduction viii
    Understanding Individuality in Leadership x
    Cultivating a Growth Mindset xi
    Shaping the Future xii
    The Dual Reality of Today's Youth xiii
    A Personal Connection and the Power of Small Changes xiv

Chapter 1: The Leadership Equation 1
    The "X" Factor of Leadership 3
    Myth-Busters: Leadership Edition 5
    Are You Too Young to Lead? 7
    Wisdom Wrapping 10

Chapter 2: The Mirror of Self 11
    Becoming Your Own Sherlock Holmes 12
    The Jigsaw Puzzle of You 17
    Aligning Your Compass 21
    Wisdom Wrapping 23

Contents

Chapter 3: Planting Seeds of Growth 25
Unleashing the Power of "Yet" 27
Real-Life Superheroes and Their Secret Powers 32
Cultivating your inner garden 35
Wisdom Wrapping 37

Chapter 4: The Art of Bouncing Back 38
From Stumbling Blocks to Stepping Stones 39
A Critic's Guide to Constructive Feedback 42
Pressure Cooker: How to Keep Your Cool. 44
Wisdom Wrapping 48

Chapter 5: Choose Your Adventure 49
The Dangerous Allure of the Forbidden Fruit 50
The Decision-Making Map 53
Your Internal GPS: Making Choices that Matter 55
Wisdom Wrapping 58

Chapter 6: The Power of the Spoken Word 59
The ABCs of Effective Communication 60
Relationship Weaving: Threads of Conversation 63
The Subtle Art of Influencing Without Authority 64
Wisdom Wrapping 67

Chapter 7: The Art of Empathy 69
Understanding and Expressing Empathy 71
The Role of Empathy in Conflict Resolution 73
The Inclusive Leader's Handbook 76
Wisdom Wrapping 79

Chapter 8: Change Makers Among Us 80
Young Leaders: The World's Hidden Gems 82
The Ripple Effect: Creating Impact Close to Home 85
Leadership Lab: Putting Theory Into Practice 88
Wisdom Wrapping 91

Chapter 9: Unleashing Your Inner Da Vinci 92
The Leadership Palette: Blending Creativity and Innovation 94
The Light Bulb Moment: Fostering Innovative Thinking 96
From Daydreams to Reality: Executing Ideas 98
Wisdom Wrapping 102

Chapter 10: Your Journey Begins Now 103
The Start Line: From Couch to Action 106
Plotting Your Leadership Quest 107
The Power Bank: Fueling Your Motivation 109
Wisdom Wrapping 113

PREFACE

Over the past 18 years of my corporate journey which has been empowering, I've mentored more than a thousand fresh graduates and young adults. The desire to author *The Leadership Blueprint: A Guide to Brilliance for Teens and Young Adults* arose from these countless interactions and the realization that a crucial element was often missing in the development of these young minds—leadership.

Leadership isn't confined to the boundaries of a title or position; it encapsulates a set of skills, a mindset, and a life approach. It encompasses empathy, conflict resolution, innovation, and the ability to drive change. Yet, I found these crucial attributes absent in many young adults I interacted with. The gap was evident and the need to fill it was urgent. Therefore, the idea for this book was conceived.

My personal journey as a parent fueled the motivation to transform this concept into reality. I observed my son, his aspirations, dreams, and dilemmas and I desired that he grows into a strong, empathetic and innovative leader. I wanted him to be equipped to navigate the rollercoaster of life with resilience and grace. The realization dawned that my son was not alone.

Preface

There were millions of young individuals out there who could harness their leadership potential to make a difference in their lives.

Thus, this book culminates my years of corporate experience, thousands of hours spent in heart-to-heart conversations with young adults, countless interactions with parents and teachers and my personal journey as a father. It serves as a roadmap for emerging leaders ready to leave their footprints on the sands of time. It stands as a testimony to my firm belief in the inherent leadership potential of every young individual and the transformative power of leadership skills in enhancing personal and professional fulfilment.

Embarking on the leadership journey is a step that must be taken early enough. I invite you, today's young leaders, to plunge into this journey with open hearts and minds. Let's commence this exciting journey together to unearth and polish the leader within you which helps you to stay prepared. As you shape your future, you shape the world. Your journey begins now. Are you ready to step up?

INTRODUCTION

*D*ear Reader,

Leadership is a term that we often associate with executives in suits or presidents making world-changing decisions. It's easy to forget that leadership is not confined to boardrooms or parliamentary halls, nor is it a quality reserved only for those with years of experience under their belts. Regardless of age or background, it's a skill that anyone, including you, can nurture.

You might be asking yourself, "Why a book on leadership for teens and young adults?" I am glad you asked.

Over the past ten years, in addition to my leadership role within my organization, I have dedicated myself to coaching young individuals. I have had the opportunity to interact with teens and young adults brimming with vitality, passion, and the desire to make a mark in the world. Their innovative ideas, enthusiasm, and readiness to change their surroundings have always fascinated me.

Yet, in these interactions, I have also observed a trend. A lot of this boundless energy and potential feels scattered. I've seen teens juggling school, sports, hobbies, volunteering, and social life—each activity like a separate world, with no connection to the others. I've seen young adults switching between college, part-time jobs, passion projects, and relationships, trying to excel in all but often feeling like they are not genuinely succeeding.

Consider Alex, a teen I coached a few years ago. Alex was a diligent student, a budding artist, a volunteer at the local community centre, and a part-time waiter at a café. He was enthusiastic and committed to each role. Still, he often told me how he felt like he was in a whirlwind, constantly switching gears, and never really leading in any area. This is a sentiment I've heard from many young individuals.

As a leader in my organization, I have often witnessed young newcomers bristling with potential yet feeling lost when thrust into leadership roles. They need clarity and a solid foundation of what it means to lead and how to do it effectively.

This is why I am writing this book. By understanding leadership early on, teens and young adults can channel their energy more effectively, creating a synergy in their various roles rather than feeling torn between them. Leadership isn't just about guiding a team in a corporate environment; it's about making decisions, taking responsibility, influencing others positively, standing up for what you believe is right, and leading your own life.

My goal isn't to turn you into a CEO or a world leader overnight. Leadership is a journey that takes time, practice, resilience, and a readiness to learn from both successes and setbacks. However, starting this journey early on can give you a significant advantage.

Through this book, I aim to provide you with the tools to develop your leadership skills. Drawing from my own experiences, those of other leaders who started their journey at a young age, and the lessons I've learned from coaching young individuals, I hope to offer you valuable insights, practical tips, and real-life examples to guide your journey.

It's more than just leading others; it's about leading your life with purpose and direction. So, are you ready to take the reins and embark on this exciting journey? Let's get started.

Understanding Individuality in Leadership

Throughout this book, I want to clarify one thing: I am not here to overhaul your lifestyle or ask you to fundamentally change who you are. The teen and young adult years are a time of exploration and self-discovery. It's when you delve into different activities, hobbies, interests, and relationships to figure out who you are and want to be. I respect this journey and the individuality that comes with it.

We all have unique personalities and strengths. Some of us are introverts who excel in solitary pursuits and deep thinking. In contrast, others are extroverts who thrive in social situations and group activities. Some of us are logical thinkers, while others are creative spirits. Each one of these traits brings value to the table and can contribute to becoming a successful leader.

Take, for example, Lily, a naturally introverted teenager I coached. She initially felt that her reserved nature would hinder leadership, which she thought was the domain of the outspoken and charismatic. However, as Lily began to understand the essence of leadership, she realized that her ability to listen attentively, think deeply, and communicate thoughtfully were all assets to her leadership potential.

Leadership isn't about becoming someone else; it's about becoming the best version of yourself.

Cultivating a Growth Mindset

As you read through this book, my main request is for you to embrace a growth mindset without changing who you are. Carol Dweck, a psychologist, coined the term "growth mindset" to describe the belief that we can develop our abilities and intelligence through hard work, learning, and perseverance.

It's about understanding that challenges are growth opportunities, that effort is a pathway to mastery, and that criticism is a valuable source of feedback. It's about recognizing that you're a work in progress; every step you take is a step towards becoming better.

This mindset can act as your compass, guiding you via the ups and downs of your leadership journey. It can help you see the value in every experience, whether it be acing an exam, flubbing a presentation, scoring the winning goal, or experiencing a tough breakup. These experiences come with lessons that can help you grow, not just as a leader but as a person.

Remember Alex from earlier? Once he adopted a growth mindset, he started viewing his varied roles not as separate, clashing responsibilities but as different avenues for learning and developing leadership skills. His academic pursuits improved his problem-solving abilities, his art cultivated creativity, his volunteering nurtured empathy, and his part-time job enhanced his time-management skills. By shifting his perspective slightly, Alex could bring his scattered worlds together, leading to synergy rather than chaos.

My goal with this book is to help you harness your potential and to turn your daily activities and passions into opportunities for growth and leadership. Whether you're an introvert or an extrovert, a thinker or a dreamer, a bookworm or a sports enthusiast, there's a leader within you waiting to emerge.

The journey to leadership doesn't require drastic changes but minor tweaks in mindset and focus. These small tweaks can ultimately lead to significant personal growth and success.

Shaping the Future

In writing this book, I am motivated by my experiences and a pressing realization: that today's teens and young adults, including you, my dear reader, are the stewards of our future. The decisions you make, the actions you take, and the leaders you become will shape the world for the next 80 years or more.

We live in an era of significant challenges—climate change, social inequality, political unrest, technological disruptions, and a global pandemic, to name a few. The consequences of these challenges have shaped your lives in ways that no generation before you have experienced. However, every challenge presents an opportunity and your age, with its resilience, innovation, and spirit, has the potential to re-direct these challenges into opportunities for change.

Consider the climate change movement, a global effort led predominantly by young individuals. The name, Greta Thunberg, a teenager from Sweden, has become synonymous with this fight. Despite her young age, she has inspired millions worldwide, demonstrating that leadership has no age limit.

You don't need to be a world-renowned activist to make a difference. As a leader, even your small choices can significantly impact you. Whether standing up against bullying in your school, organizing a community cleanup, leading a group project in college, or starting a business that solves a local problem, you can influence your surroundings meaningfully.

My motivation in writing this book is to help you harness this power. By developing your leadership skills, you can channel your energy, passions, ideas, and potential to not just navigate the challenges of the present but to shape the future.

As you embark on this leadership journey, remember that you're not just leading for yourself. You're leading for your community, your nation, and your world.

The Dual Reality of Today's Youth

While today's teens and young adults face challenges, they also confront personal struggles that can hinder their potential. One issue that deeply concerns me is the rising trend of unhealthy lifestyle habits among young people. These habits pose significant health risks and impede their ability to thrive and lead.

In my coaching sessions, I've seen the damaging impact of poor lifestyle choices on bright young individuals. It's heartbreaking to see such immense potential clouded by detrimental habits. Leadership skills can play a pivotal role in helping young people make better decisions, resist unhealthy influences, and maintain a positive lifestyle.

On the other hand, I've also witnessed young individuals' remarkable creativity and innovation. From developing novel apps that address everyday problems to initiating social enterprises that drive community development and launching environmental campaigns that protect our planet, their ideas and initiatives are truly inspiring.

Consider Jack, a young man I coached who turned his interest in technology and social service into a successful initiative. He created a platform that connects volunteers with various community service opportunities, fostering a spirit of volunteerism and creating a positive societal impact. Jack's venture demonstrated his leadership skills and civic confidence: the ability to turn an idea into reality, unite a team towards a common goal, and positively influence his community.

This dichotomy of personal struggles and inspiring potential is what makes the journey of today's young leaders complex yet rewarding. In this book, I aim to help you navigate these challenges and harness your potential to lead a healthier, more fulfilling life and positively impact your world.

A Personal Connection and the Power of Small Changes

Two decades ago, I was in your shoes. I remember the excitement, the confusion, the dreams, and the doubts that come with being a teen and a young adult. I remember juggling academics, hobbies, and relationships, trying to figure out who I was and what I wanted to become. I understand what you're going through and so, I am here.

I am not here to preach, to dictate, or to impose. I am here to tell you that small changes in your daily life can yield significant results. I am here to guide you in making minor tweaks and cultivating habits and skills that can transform your life.

Leadership is not about grand gestures or earth-shattering decisions. More often than not, it's about the small actions we take every day. It's about how we treat ourselves and others, handle failure, react to success, approach problems, and learn and grow.

By refining these small actions, you can build a better relationship with yourself, understand your strengths and weaknesses, and cultivate self-respect that isn't swayed by external opinions. You can nurture healthier relationships with your family and friends, understanding their perspectives, respecting their individuality, and influencing them positively. You can contribute positively to your society, standing up for what's right, initiating change, and inspiring others to do the same. And ultimately, you can help shape a better world, one small action at a time.

This book is about helping you make these small but powerful changes. It's about turning the scattered energy of your teens and young adult years into focused potential. It's about helping you become not just a better leader but a better person.

CHAPTER 1

THE LEADERSHIP EQUATION

*D*id you ever imagine as a child that you could be a superhero? Maybe you had an imaginary cape, a secret lair, or an invisible jet. Perhaps you dreamed of saving the world or having superhuman powers. Well, guess what? You still can. I am not referring to abilities such as jumping over tall buildings in one jump or emitting laser beams from your eyes. I'm talking about a real-life superpower—leadership.

When we think about superheroes, we usually focus on their extraordinary abilities. Yet, what truly sets them apart is their leadership—their capacity to inspire, their courage to take the initiative, and their dedication to making a difference. These qualities become even more crucial in our real-world, devoid of capes and cosmic threats. And unlike fictional superpowers, anyone can develop leadership at any age.

Leadership is like a puzzle, a thrilling and complex one. There's no single way to solve it; the pieces come together differently for everyone. However, some elements form the core of the leadership puzzle, details often overlooked in the pursuit of authority and control.

In this chapter, we will unravel the mystery of this puzzle together. We'll start by discussing the true essence of leadership and bust some common myths that could cloud your understanding. Finally, we'll explore an intriguing question, "Are you too young to lead?"

So, are you ready to embark on this journey? Are you ready to discover the leadership superhero within you? If you answer "yes," let's dive in because your adventure starts here.

The "X" Factor of Leadership

Picture a typical blockbuster movie. Usually, there's this unsung hero, often the underdog, who rises above all odds and saves the day. Have you ever wondered what makes these characters so compelling? It's not their size, experience, or unique abilities. It's something we're going to call the "X" factor. The "X" factor in leadership isn't about charisma, power, or status. Instead, it's about influence and impact.

Imagine a choir where each member is singing in harmony with the others. There's no visible leader, but there is one voice that subtly stands out, lifting the others and guiding them through the melody. That voice doesn't overpower the others; it only empowers them. This ability to influence and empower, without command or coercion, is leadership's "X" factor.

Yet, our society often gets caught in the trap of traditional leadership representations. You know the ones—the senior executive in a crisp suit, the political leader making rousing speeches, or the team captain calling the shots. Of course, these are forms of leadership but they're not the only ones. Leadership isn't just about leading troops into battle or commanding a boardroom. It's about creating an impact that resonates, influences, and inspires.

Let's dive deeper into this "X" factor by analyzing a few real-life scenarios.

Remember that group project you had in school where one of you, not necessarily the one appointed as the group leader, took the initiative to organize the tasks, listened to everyone's ideas, and ensured the team completed the project on time? That's the

"X" factor in action. Or recall the last time you saw someone stand up against bullying. They might not have been the strongest or the most popular but they influenced others with courage and maybe even changed how their peers viewed bullying. That's the "X" factor, too.

You might even find the "X" factor in a younger sibling who manages to get the whole family—despite everyone's busy schedules—to play a game together, not by demanding or dictating, but by inspiring and motivating. The individuals may not have held a formal title or authority in these examples, yet they demonstrated leadership. They influenced those around them and created a positive impact. They exercised the "X" factor.

Why is this so important for you, today's teens and young adults? It's because understanding this "X" factor can revolutionize the way you view leadership. You start to see that leadership is open to more than just a corporate office or a government building. It's everywhere and in every interaction and action that influences others and makes a difference.

Most importantly, it's within you. Yes, you have this "X" factor. It's in how you help a friend in need, contribute to your community, or inspire your peers with passion and dedication. You may not always see it, but it's there, waiting to be nurtured and unleashed.

By realizing this, you can get older, have a particular title, or achieve a certain status to become a leader. You can start right here, right now. You can begin by identifying opportunities in your daily life to influence others positively and make a difference. Every day, you have many moments where you can exercise your "X" factor: when you stand up for what is right, even when it's unpopular.

When you support others in their goals and aspirations, offering encouragement and assistance, you foster a spirit of collaboration and empowerment.

Myth-Busters: Leadership Edition

Let's embark on an exciting journey of debunking some popular myths about leadership. Similar to how detectives in your favourite mystery novels untangle the most intricate riddles, we're about to decipher and discard some misguided beliefs. By doing so, we'll shed light on the genuine meaning of leadership which is unclouded by misconceptions.

Myth 1: Leadership equals authority

Let's take a quick trip back to ancient Rome, to the Colosseum, where gladiators fight for power. Leadership, however, is about something other than being the last one standing in the arena. It isn't about holding the sceptre of authority or commanding obedience. Leadership is about influence, not control. It's about inspiring others to pursue a common goal, not ruling over them.

Myth 2: Leaders are born, not made

Some people believe that leadership is a trait only a few are born with. This belief is as fanciful as a unicorn prancing over a rainbow! Leadership is not a trait that magically appears in one's DNA. It's a set of skills and attitudes that can be learned and nurtured, like playing an instrument or mastering a new language.

Myth 3: Leaders have all the answers

For a moment, imagine that you're on a quiz show and the host expects you to know every single answer. Sounds intimidating? Fortunately, leadership is different from this. Leaders aren't omniscient beings who know everything. Great leaders acknowledge their limitations, are not afraid to admit when they do not know something, and welcome opportunities to learn from others.

Myth 4: Leadership is a solo act

Picture a lone wolf, which is separated from the pack, howling at the moon. The lone wolf may look majestic, but its isolation emphasizes the vital role of collaboration and community in effective leadership. Leadership is far from a solo act. It is about collaboration and fostering a sense of community. It's about appreciating each team member's unique strengths and leveraging them towards a common goal.

Myth 5: You're too young to lead

This myth is the most dangerous because it discourages young people like you from recognizing and developing your leadership potential. Imagine telling Mozart he was too young to compose music or Malala Yousafzai she was too young to stand up for girls' education. Age is not a measure of leadership capability. Your ideas, your passion, and your determination are the things that make you a leader.

> YOUR IDEAS, YOUR PASSION, AND YOUR DETERMINATION ARE THE THINGS THAT MAKE YOU A LEADER.

By busting these myths, we bring to light the true essence of leadership. Leadership isn't about being the loudest in the room or holding the highest rank. It's neither a trait you're born with nor requires you to know everything or go it alone. And indeed, it's not restricted by age.

So, where does this leave us? With the understanding that regardless of your age or experience, you have the potential to be a leader. Leadership is an exciting journey that involves learning, growing, and, most importantly, influencing others positively.

Remember, leadership is like a musical instrument. Anyone can learn to play it, but only those who practice diligently, learn from mistakes and play passionately create beautiful music. Let's tune our leadership instruments and start making some harmonious impact!

Are You Too Young to Lead?

If I handed you the keys to a time machine and told you to travel back to your favourite era in history, you'd be thrilled. Imagine the possibilities—strolling among dinosaurs, observing the construction of the pyramids, or perhaps witnessing the signing of the Declaration of Independence.

Now, what if I asked you to spot the leaders in each of these scenarios? You might naturally think of the chief of the tribe, the pharaoh, or the Founding Fathers as classic examples of leaders. However, true leadership can often be found in unexpected places. Consider a young shepherd confidently guiding and protecting his flock, a young apprentice skillfully coordinating and inspiring his fellow workers, or a young patriot passionately rallying his peers towards a common cause. Leadership is not confined to specific roles or titles; it is a matter of perspective. Sometimes, we may overlook potential leaders because we only focus on well-known figures. However, by broadening our viewpoint, we can recognize leadership in individuals who may not fit the conventional mould. It's time to shift our perspective and appreciate the leaders among us, hidden in the ordinary and extraordinary moments of everyday life.

There's a persistent belief in many societies that youth is a barrier to leadership. The misconception that leadership is the prerogative of the old and experienced is as old as history. But the question we're tackling here concerns something other than age but ability, passion, and influence.

Let's break down this concept with a few real-life examples:

Greta Thunberg: At just 15, Ms. Greta started a global movement against climate change, inspiring millions worldwide to take action. She got a PhD in Environmental Science and became the CEO of an environmental organization. She saw a problem, felt passionate about it, and took action to resolve the issue.

Malala Yousafzai: As a young girl, Ms. Malala fought for her right to go to school in a place where girls were not allowed to do so. Despite facing life-threatening obstacles, she continued to fight for girls' education worldwide, ultimately becoming the youngest Nobel Prize laureate.

Mozart: This musical prodigy started composing symphonies when most kids his age were learning to tie their shoelaces. His leadership in music continues to influence and inspire musicians centuries after his death.

These examples illuminate one crucial fact—leadership isn't about age but influence. These young leaders might have had only a few decades of experience, but they had the vision, courage, and ability to inspire others. They debunk the myth that leadership is a function of age and demonstrate that leadership is about making a difference.

So, are you too young to lead? The resounding answer is "no." You are always young enough to inspire, make a difference, and be a leader.

Being a teen or young adult today is like being a pioneer on the cusp of a thrilling adventure. You're at an age where your mind is buzzing with ideas, your heart is full of passion, and your spirit is eager to make a mark in the world. Now is the perfect time to use these qualities to your advantage and become a star.

You don't need to lead a global movement or win a Nobel Prize to be considered a leader (though if you do, that's pretty awesome!). You can demonstrate leadership in everyday scenarios—standing up for what you believe in, supporting a friend in need, or taking the initiative in school or community projects.

Embrace that you're young, full of potential, and capable of leading. Start where you are, use what you have, and do what you can. You'll find that, with time, you're not just a leader to your peers but also to yourself.

Remember, age is just a number but influence is limitless. You're ready to lead if you have a cause you're passionate about, a vision you want to share, and the courage to take the first step.

Wisdom Wrapping

As we close the curtain on this enlightening exploration into the world of leadership, we hope to have sparked a flame of understanding and curiosity in your young minds. We went on a trip together through the ever-changing world of leadership. We looked at its many sides, busted some myths, and realized that being a leader has nothing to do with age.

We unveiled the mystery of the elusive "X" factor, revealing that it's not about authority or control but rather about influence and impact. During our journey to debunk myths, we faced the giants of misinformation and found that leadership is not a privilege of birth, age, or standing. It is, instead, an ability that can be taught, practised, and mastered.

The most crucial revelation was acknowledging that you, our youthful reader, can now step up to the leadership plate. With numerous real-life examples, we demonstrated that age is not a barrier but a launchpad for leadership.

Let's carry these revelations with us as we turn the page to the next chapter. Let's imbue each of our actions with the understanding that we can create an impact, regardless of our age or life stage. Remember, leadership is not a distant dream but a present reality waiting for you to seize it.

CHAPTER 2

THE MIRROR OF SELF

*I*n this chapter, we'll venture on a journey of self-discovery, aiming to understand ourselves better. In the same way, a mirror shows us how we look; introspection allows us to see our inner selves—our strengths, weaknesses, passions, and values. Let's delve deeper and uncover the real 'you,' piece together your unique jigsaw puzzle, and align your compass for life's journey.

Becoming Your Own Sherlock Holmes

For a moment, imagine stepping into the worn-in yet remarkably comfortable shoes of the world's greatest detective, Sherlock Holmes. You find yourself wandering through the cobblestone streets of London, shrouded in a thick, velvety fog. The city is a maze of puzzles, and you're about to solve the most intricate one yet—the enigma that is you.

Don't worry; this doesn't involve crime scenes or convoluted plots of Moriarty. Instead, this case demands the same astuteness and keen observation that Sherlock employs. And in doing so, you'll transform from an enigma into an open book, waiting to be read and understood.

Let's start with the tools of our investigation. Sherlock has his magnifying glass and mind palace, but we have something even more profound—introspection and self-reflection. These tools aren't found in any detective kit but reside within us. They are ready to be used to keep track of our ideas, feelings, and reactions to the world around us.

Your first case should be identifying your strengths. Remember when Sherlock played his violin to think better? That's because music was one of his strengths. Similarly, think about what you excel in. Is it solving mathematical problems or painting a picture that speaks a thousand words? Or is it how you can quickly initiate a conversation with strangers?

The second case on our docket is pinpointing weaknesses. We should not focus on them negatively but understand areas where we might need improvement or support. Even Sherlock had his flaws; remember his struggles with social niceties? So, what's yours? You may find it challenging to manage your time effectively or perhaps public speaking makes you slightly nervous.

The third case requires digging deeper to uncover your values and passions. What stirs your heart and fuels your spirit? It might be a tricky case, but it's worth solving. After all, these are the aspects that will guide your leadership journey.

Lastly, we must identify our goals and the dreams we wish to chase. Sherlock had his pursuit of truth and justice. What's yours? Is it leading a technological revolution or becoming a champion for the environment?

Like any good detective, remember to keep an open mind throughout this investigation. Gather your clues without judgment. Remember, every strength, weakness, value, goal, or passion you uncover is a piece of the puzzle that makes you unique.

By the end of this self-investigation, you'll have your personal 'case file,' a blueprint of who you are. You'll be surprised at what you find. You'll see your strengths in a new light and realize that your weaknesses are merely growth opportunities, your values will guide your actions, and your goals will motivate your journey.

The game is afoot, young detectives. Take out your magnifying glasses and start exploring.

After all, as Sherlock said, "There is nothing more deceptive than an obvious fact," and there's nothing more deceptive yet revealing than understanding oneself. Let's decipher the mystery of 'You' together.

> UNDERSTANDING ONESELF IS AKIN TO HAVING A DETAILED MAP WHEN NAVIGATING THROUGH THE OFTEN-CONFUSING LANDSCAPE OF LIFE AND LEADERSHIP.

Embarking on this journey of self-discovery isn't merely about gathering a few fascinating insights about ourselves. This introspective adventure carries profound importance, especially when you are standing at the threshold of your leadership journey. Understanding oneself is akin to having a detailed map when navigating through the often-confusing landscape of life and leadership.

One might wonder, "Why is self-awareness so crucial?" Imagine piloting a ship without a compass or building a house without a blueprint. It would be a challenging and potentially disastrous endeavor. Similarly, attempting to grow as a leader without understanding your own strengths, weaknesses, values, and goals is like setting out on a voyage without a map.

Your self-awareness is your compass, your blueprint, and your roadmap. It guides your actions, influences your decision-making, and shapes your interactions with others. Knowing your strengths allows you to lead from a place of confidence, harnessing what you naturally excel at to create impact. Recognizing your weaknesses isn't about self-criticism but about understanding areas where you can learn, grow, and seek help from others.

Understanding your values provides a moral and ethical framework for your leadership. They are your guiding principles, the 'non-negotiables' of what you stand for. Identifying your goals gives your leadership journey direction. They are the milestones you strive for, the change you want to bring about in your world.

Furthermore, self-awareness also promotes empathy and understanding towards others. Recognizing our own strengths and weaknesses can help us appreciate the diversity of skills and talents in our teams. Understanding our own values and goals can make us more respectful of the values and goals of others.

Being self-aware is not a one-time task but a continuous process, a habit of self-reflection that we cultivate over time. It's like a mirror that we return to, again and again, to check our alignment, make necessary adjustments, and ensure we're on the right path. As we grow and evolve, our self-understanding, too, will change and deepen, leading to more profound insights and greater wisdom. So, the question isn't really whether you should become your own Sherlock Holmes, but rather, can you afford not to?

By fully understanding ourselves, we can lead with authenticity, lead with empathy, and ultimately, lead with impact. So, let's continue our self-exploration, one clue at a time.

EXERCISE SHEET 1

Becoming Your Own Sherlock Holmes

1. Investigate Your Strengths: List at least five things you believe you excel at. They could be specific skills, like coding or playing the piano, or general attributes, like being a good listener or quick learner.

....
....
....
....
....

2. Examine Your Weaknesses: Be honest with yourself and identify areas where you struggle. Remember, these are not faults but opportunities for growth and development.

....
....
....
....
....

3. Discover Your Values: What are the guiding principles in your life? What do you stand for? Write down your core values.

....
....
....
....
....

4. *Outline Your Goals:* What do you hope to achieve in the future? These could be short-term goals or long-term aspirations. List them down.

....
....
....
....
....

The Jigsaw Puzzle of You

Close your eyes and think of a jigsaw puzzle. Each piece, with its unique shape and design, fits perfectly with the others to create a beautiful picture. This puzzle is a metaphor for you. Each amount signifies a part of you—your strengths, weaknesses, values, passions, and goals.

Think back to the last time you assembled a jigsaw puzzle. Initially, it was just a scattered mess of individual pieces. But as you started piecing it together, a clear image began to form. Similarly, we've gathered various information about ourselves in our Sherlockian investigation. Now, it's time to start putting them together.

Your strengths and passions form the corner pieces of this puzzle. These pieces are relatively easy to fit into place. Your passion might be music, writing, coding, or athletics. You may be a pro at problem-solving, a great listener, or a natural at making people laugh. These corner pieces lay the foundation for your puzzle and give you the initial direction.

Your weaknesses, on the other hand, might seem like those frustrating middle pieces. You know the ones – the pieces that you can't seem to fit in anywhere. But remember, no puzzle is complete without them. They are opportunities disguised as challenges. Perhaps you struggle with organization or have a fear of public speaking. These aren't mistakes that we should be covered up; they're aspects to be understood and worked upon.

Your values and goals are the edge pieces forming the framework of your puzzle. These are your non-negotiables, your guiding principles, the things you stand for, and the milestones you're striving towards. They provide direction and structure to your life and leadership.

> YOUR VALUES AND GOALS ARE THE EDGE PIECES FORMING THE FRAMEWORK OF YOUR PUZZLE.

Like in a puzzle, every piece has a role and a specific place to fit. Your strengths allow you to excel and bring unique contributions to your team. Acknowledging your weaknesses makes room for growth and collaboration. Staying true to your values brings authenticity to your leadership, and chasing your goals keeps you motivated and driven.

And, of course, you can remember the puzzle's image, the complete picture that all these pieces come together to form. That's the unique 'You.' As a whole, you are greater than the sum of these individual pieces. You are a distinctive combination of strengths, weaknesses, passions, values, and goals, making you the leader only you can be. It's important to remember that this puzzle will take time to come together. It takes time, patience, and perseverance. You might have to rearrange some pieces as you grow and evolve. But this jigsaw puzzle's beauty is that there must be a 'wrong' way to assemble it. It's what makes it unique to you.

Assembling the jigsaw puzzle of 'You' is a personal and profound journey. It's a journey of understanding, acceptance, and growth. It's about celebrating your strengths, acknowledging your weaknesses, standing firm on your values, and relentlessly pursuing your goals.

Ultimately, you'll know who you are and what you want to be. And with this self-understanding, you'll be ready to step into the world of leadership, embracing your unique style and making a difference in your own way. So, let's put these pieces together and complete the beautiful jigsaw puzzle 'You.'

 EXERCISE SHEET 2

The Jigsaw Puzzle of You

1. *Assemble Your Strengths:* Using the strengths you listed in the previous exercise, find examples from your life where you have effectively used these strengths.

....
....
....
....
....

2. Fit in Your Weaknesses: Now, take the weaknesses you've identified and consider ways to work on them. How could you turn these weaknesses into strengths?

....
....
....
....

3. Frame Your Values: Reflect on your values. Why are they important to you? How do they influence your decisions and actions?

....
....
....
....

4. Place Your Goals: Revisit your goals. Why do you want to achieve them? What do you have to do to get there?

....
....
....
....

Aligning Your Compass

Imagine you are an intrepid explorer, standing at the edge of an exciting and uncharted territory, ready to step into the unknown. What's the one thing you'd need the most? That's right, a compass.

But this is not just any compass. This personal compass is a vital tool that will help you find your way through the rough spots of life and leadership.

You might be asking, "What is a personal compass?" Essentially, it's an internal guidance system culminating in your strengths, weaknesses, values, and goals. It shows what you want your life to be like and who you are. Like an accurate compass, it helps you stay oriented and navigate the challenges you may encounter.

Now, how do we align this personal compass? You've already done a lot of the groundwork. The process of self-discovery, becoming your own Sherlock Holmes, and piecing together the jigsaw puzzle of 'You' has prepared the elements you need to calibrate your personal compass.

Let's start with north—your guiding principle. This is what you value the most. It could be integrity, compassion, creativity, or perseverance. This value is your true north, guiding your decisions and actions, ensuring you remain authentic to who you are.

Next is south—your primary goal. What is the milestone you're striving towards? It could be becoming an entrepreneur, driving social change, or writing a best-selling novel. This goal gives your journey a clear destination and motivates you during challenging times.

Moving on to east—your crucial strength. This is something you excel in and can rely on to overcome obstacles and drive impact. You may be an excellent communicator, a problem-solver, or a creative thinker. This strength is your trusted tool, ready to be deployed when needed.

Lastly, we have west—your acknowledged weakness. This is an area you're aware requires improvement or support. It could be time management, public speaking, or delegating tasks. Recognizing this weakness isn't a setback; it's an opportunity for growth and collaboration.

Your Personal Compass is aligned once you've identified your North, South, East, and West. But remember, using this compass requires honesty and courage. It's about being truthful to who you are and having the bravery to follow your path, even when it's the road less travelled.

Aligning and following your personal compass will be challenging. There will be times when you lose your way or face obstacles that seem too daunting. But remember, every challenge is an opportunity for growth. In these moments, your compass is crucial, reminding you of who you are and what you aspire to be.

EXERCISE SHEET 3: ALIGNING YOUR COMPASS

1. *Identify Your True North:* Which of the values you listed earlier resonates the most with you? This is your guiding principle, your true north.

....
....
....
....
....

2. *Mark Your South:* Choose the most crucial goal from your list. This is your primary goal, your south.

....

3. *Find Your East:* What strength do you rely on the most? This strength is your east.

4. *Acknowledge Your West:* Which weakness are you most motivated to work on? This weakness is your west.

Wisdom Wrapping

The journey of leadership is exciting and challenging in equal measure. And just like an explorer stepping into uncharted territories, you'll face your fair share of unknowns and uncertainties. But with your compass in hand, you'll be ready to navigate through these challenges, making decisions aligned with who you are and what you stand for.

So, hold your personal compass high and step into the exciting leadership journey. Remember, the purpose is not to reach a destination quickly but to grow, learn, and positively impact. So, let's start this journey together, guided by our personal compass and driven by the passion to lead.

CHAPTER 3

PLANTING SEEDS OF GROWTH

*J*ust like a tiny seed that needs the right conditions to grow into a mighty tree, you, too, dear reader, have the potential to grow beyond your wildest dreams. All you need are apt conditions and a little nurturing. This chapter is dedicated to helping you cultivate those conditions, watering that seed within you and encouraging it to sprout.

Growth, however, is only sometimes a linear process. It's not a highway but a twisting, turning path filled with ups and downs. Sometimes, you might feel like you're not growing at all. However, remember that sowing seed is the first step and that growth will take time.

Itʋs increasing silently under the soil before it finally breaks through, reaching the sun. This is called the power of «Yet.»

Moreover, you're not alone in this journey. Just like superheroes have their mentors, so will you. This chapter will introduce you to real-life superheroes who, just like you, started as seeds and grew into towering trees, sharing their secret powers and how they cultivated them.

Finally, we'll delve into nurturing your inner garden, ensuring you provide the proper care and nutrients for your seed to flourish. Growth is about achieving goals and developing the right mindset, attitude, and resilience to become the best version of yourself.

So, are you ready to plant your seeds of growth, nurturing them into mighty trees of potential? Let's begin this journey together, uncovering the power of "Yet," learning from real-life superheroes, and cultivating your inner garden.

Are you prepared to sow the seeds of development, tending them until they blossom into trees of extraordinary potential? Let's embark on this adventure together, where we'll understand the significance of "Yet," study the lives of actual superheroes, and tend to our gardens of self-improvement.

Unleashing the Power of "Yet"

Are you ready to unlock a secret that has the potential to change your perspective towards growth and learning? Well, let's dive into it. It involves a small word, just three letters, but its power is truly magical. That word, dear reader, is "Yet."

Picture this: You've been trying to master a complex mathematical concept. You've spent hours pouring over the textbook, trying to decode the language of numbers and symbols, but it's just not clicking.

Frustration bubbles up, and you say, "I can't understand this."

Let's tweak that statement: "I can't understand this...yet."

Did you feel that? That subtle shift from despair to possibility, from a full stop to an ellipsis, indicates continuity. This is called the power of "Yet." It acknowledges the present struggle but also keeps the window of potential wide open.

"Yet" is the bridge that connects our present with our future potential. It's an admission that while we may not possess a skill or understand a concept now, it doesn't mean we won't be able to in the future. It shifts our focus from a fixed mindset, the belief that one's innate talents are fixed, to a growth mindset, the conviction that one's talents are skills that can be brushed through practice and dedication.

A well-known psychologist, Carol Dweck, spent much time investigating the role "Yet" plays in the growth mindset.

People with a growth mindset, as she describes them, are eager to take on new tasks, resilient in the face of adversity, aware that hard work is the key to success, open to constructive criticism, and motivated by the achievements of others.

Applying the power of "Yet" is like planting a seed in your brain. Each time you encounter a challenge, it's like watering that seed. With patience, persistence, and the right mindset, that seed of "Yet" can grow into a mighty tree of capability.

Remember, dear reader, "Yet" does not imply immediate success. It's not about winning every time or being perfect right off the bat. It's about embracing the journey of learning, making mistakes, and growing from them. It's about recognizing that struggle is an essential part of the process, not a signal of defeat.

> IT'S ABOUT RECOGNIZING THAT STRUGGLE IS AN ESSENTIAL PART OF THE PROCESS, NOT A SIGNAL OF DEFEAT.

Thomas Edison, the inventor of the light bulb, once famously stated, "I have not failed. I just found ten thousand ways that won't work."

If he had given up after a few tries, we might not have the electric light bulb today! Edison embraced the power of "yet," and his persistence eventually paid off. Embracing the power of "yet" can transform your life. It turns challenges into opportunities for learning, failures into stepping stones for success, and dreams into achievable goals. It encourages you to persevere, innovate, and grow.

So, the next time you hit a roadblock, add that magic word to your speech.

Instead of saying, "I can't do this," say, "I can't do this...yet."

That's all for now, dear reader. Remember, you're on a journey of growth and learning. It might be challenging, but it's also exciting and filled with infinite potential. And whenever you're in doubt, remember the power of "yet." After all, you're not there...yet!

One must remember the importance of taking risks in growth and learning. You see, stepping out of your comfort zone and taking personal risks is like fertilizing your growth. It may feel scary or uncomfortable, just as a seed might feel the pressure as it pushes its way out of the soil. But just as the seed needs to break through the soil to reach the sunlight, you must take risks to reach your potential.

Embracing the power of "yet" can be an empowering ally in this journey. When faced with a challenging task or an ambitious project, you might think, "This is too hard. I'm not ready to take this on." However, remember our magic word and say, "I'm not ready to take this on...yet." This simple tweak in your language can create a world of difference. It implies that you're open to learning and willing to take that leap of faith, not knowing whether you'll land on your feet. You grow when you push your limits, are willing to fail, and learn from your mistakes.

Similarly, when setting goals for yourself, don't limit yourself to what you know you can achieve. Go ahead and set 'stretching' goals—ones that push you to your limits and beyond. When these goals seem too daunting, remember, you may not be able to achieve them...yet. But with persistence, hard work, and a growth mindset, you will be surprised by how far you can go.

Stretching goals challenge you to break free from your limiting beliefs and venture into the unknown. They demand that you keep learning and keep growing. Each stretching goal is like a new adventure, a new journey towards a better version of yourself.

Remember, the sweetest fruit often lies just beyond our reach. You might not be able to reach it...yet. But with every attempt and stretch, you're growing taller, stronger, and capable of reaching that fruit.

So, whether it's about taking personal risks or setting stretching goals, remember to embrace the power of "yet." It's your compass guiding you towards growth, your beacon lighting up the path of learning, your magic word turning impossibilities into possibilities. Remember, you're a work in progress and every setback, every failure, every risk, every stretch is a stepping stone to a better you.

📋 EXERCISE 1 - UNLEASHING THE POWER OF "YET"

1. Identify three things you believe you're not good at or can't do. Write them down.

....
....
....
....
....

2. Now, add the word "yet" to the end of each statement.

....
....
....
....
....

3. Write down three steps you could take to work towards improving each area.

....
....
....
....
....

4. Reflect on this exercise. How does adding "yet" change your perspective on these challenges?

....
....

Real-Life Superheroes and Their Secret Powers

Every comic book or superhero movie sees a common trope—a hero, often born in ordinary circumstances, discovering their unique powers and learning to use them for the greater good. Now, you might wonder, how is this relevant to your journey?

Let me tell you, real-life superheroes walk among us. These are individuals who, much like the heroes in comics, start with ordinary lives but go on to achieve extraordinary things. Their secret powers? The growth mindset, resilience, determination, and the belief in their ability to make a difference.

Consider Jack Ma. Born into an ordinary family in China, Ma faced numerous rejections early in life. He was turned down for multiple jobs, even being rejected by KFC. Before he finally passed his college entrance test, he failed it twice. He failed many times when he tried to start a business. However, Jack Ma did not let these rejections and failures define him. Instead, he saw them as stepping stones to success. Today, he has co-founded Alibaba, one of the world's largest e-commerce platforms. His secret power? Resilience in the face of failure.

Next, we have Michelle Obama. Born in a working-class family in Chicago's South Side, she faced many challenges related to her race and socioeconomic status. However, she didn't let these challenges stop her from pursuing her dreams. She excelled academically and went on to study at Princeton University and Harvard Law School. Later, as the First Lady of the United States, she used her platform to advocate for causes like education, health, and military families. She turned her struggles into strengths, inspiring millions worldwide with grace, resilience, and authenticity. Michelle Obama's secret power? The belief is that her voice and actions can make a difference.

Then, we have Elon Musk, a man who's aiming for the stars, quite literally. An immigrant from South Africa, Musk revolutionised multiple industries, from electric cars to space travel. Musk faced numerous failures and was even on the verge of bankruptcy. But did he give up? No. He embraced the power of "yet" and persevered. Today, he's paving the way for the future of humanity. Musk's ability? Unyielding perseverance and an unquenchable thirst for innovation.

These real-life superheroes show us that everyone has the potential to make a difference.

> ALL YOU NEED IS THE BELIEF IN YOUR ABILITY TO GROW, THE COURAGE TO FACE CHALLENGES HEAD-ON, AND THE PERSEVERANCE TO KEEP GOING, NO MATTER WHAT.

You don't need a cape or superhuman strength. All you need is the belief in your ability to grow, the courage to face challenges head-on, and the perseverance to keep going, no matter what.

So, the next time you have a problem or failure, remember this. Think of these real-life superheroes. They, too, faced obstacles. They, too, had moments of self-doubt. But they tapped into their secret powers, embraced the growth mindset, and transformed their challenges into stepping stones to success. Remember, superheroes are not born. They are made. And who's to say the next superhero isn't reading these lines right now? It could be you.

 EXERCISE 2 - REAL-LIFE SUPERHEROES AND THEIR SECRET POWERS

1. Choose three people who you consider your real-life superheroes. They could be famous personalities, community members, or even family members.

....
....
....
....
....

2. Identify the "secret powers" or strengths of each of these individuals that make them inspiring for you.

....
....
....
....
....

3. Reflect on how you can emulate these strengths in your own life.

....

Cultivating your inner garden

Imagine you are a gardener. You have a piece of land that is rich and full of possibilities. You also have different seeds, each representing another skill or quality. It's up to you now. What do you want your yard to look like? What do you want it to produce?

As we start our journey of self-growth, this is something to think about. Your thoughts, deeds, and habits are the seeds in your mind's garden. With the proper care and work, you can grow a garden inside of you that blooms with traits like leadership, resilience, empathy, and creativity.

Let's start by talking about how to care for your seeds. There are many ways to learn and grow in the world. Whether you're reading a book, going to a workshop, trying out a new sport, or working on a complex project at school or work, each is a chance to grow your seeds of potential. You might not see results immediately, but remember our magic word, "yet." You may not be able to see them yet, but if you keep caring for them and are patient, they will start to grow.

Next, let's talk about pulling weeds. Weeds are bad habits and thoughts that can stop you from growing. The bugs that can destroy your growth include putting things off, fearing failing, or comparing yourself to others. As a farmer, you need to know what these plants are and eliminate them. Remember that pulling weeds is a process that goes on all the time and takes effort and awareness.

> YOUR INNER GARDEN CAN BENEFIT SIGNIFICANTLY FROM AN UPBEAT ATTITUDE.

Lastly, remember that every garden needs a little light, which is what positivity is. Your inner garden can benefit significantly from an upbeat attitude. It's like the sun which gives your plants the energy they need to grow. When you're having trouble, look at it as a chance to learn. When you fail, tell yourself that it's just a step on the way to success.

 EXERCISE 3 - CULTIVATING YOUR INNER GARDEN

1. Reflect on your "inner garden." Identify three "seeds" or qualities you want to grow in your garden. Write them down.

....

....

....

....

....

2. Identify any "weeds" or negative habits/attitudes hindering your growth. Write down at least two and the steps you will take to pull them out.

....

....

3. Plan how you will nurture your seeds and keep your garden healthy. This could be through specific actions, developing a positive mindset, or committing to a continuous learning journey.

Remember, these exercises are not one-time activities. They are meant to be revisited and revised as you progress. As your inner garden grows and changes, so should your responses to these exercises. Happy cultivating!

Wisdom Wrapping

Being your gardener gives you a lot of freedom. It gives you the power to decide how you grow and change. What kind of plant you grow inside yourself depends on the decisions you make, how hard you work, and how you feel about things.

So, start growing your inner garden today. Your garden of skills, traits, and potential will increase if you take care of your seeds, pull out the weeds, and let the sun in. Your trip may not always be easy, and the results of your work may only sometimes be apparent immediately. But remember, you're not just growing a garden; you're growing as a person and leader.

Remember that you're in charge. What seeds are you going to plant today? What will you grow in your garden? You have a choice.

CHAPTER 4

THE ART OF BOUNCING BACK

*N*elson Mandela once said, "The greatest glory in life is not to never fall, but rather to rise every time we fall." This quote perfectly encapsulates the essence of this chapter—resilience. It's about understanding that failures, setbacks, and hurdles are not roadblocks but stepping stones on our path to growth and success.

As teenagers and young adults, you're in an exciting phase where you're stepping out of your comfort zones, learning new things, and charting your paths. While this journey is thrilling, it also comes with its challenges. You might stumble, you might fall, and that's okay. What matters is how you respond to these setbacks.

This chapter explores how to turn stumbling blocks into stepping stones, understand and accept constructive feedback, and manage stress to keep calm under pressure. Let's take the first step towards embracing resilience. Stay tuned as we delve into these topics, exploring the art of bouncing back. Remember, the key to resilience lies within you.

As the saying goes, "You're braver than you believe, stronger than you seem, and smarter than you think."

From Stumbling Blocks to Stepping Stones

Imagine you're playing a video game. You control the character, navigating different landscapes, jumping over hurdles, and overcoming challenges. Occasionally, however, you need assistance to make it through. Your character stumbles and falls, losing a life. But does the game end there? No. You respawn, learn from your past mistakes, and try again, getting better and better each time.

In many ways, life is like this video game. Your journey is filled with diverse experiences and challenges—your landscapes. Along the way, you encounter stumbling blocks. These could be a failed project, a rejected application, or a missed opportunity. Like the character in your game, you might fall. But remember, these falls aren't game-overs. They're opportunities to respawn, learn, and grow.

So, how do we turn these stumbling blocks into stepping stones? Let's delve into three key strategies:

1. **Embrace Failure:** Society often teaches us to fear failure, but we must change this perspective. Rather than perceiving failure as the antithesis of success, consider it part of the success process. Every successful person has failed numerous times on their journey. The difference is they didn't let failure deter them; they used it as fuel to keep going. Remember, it's okay to fail, but it's not okay to not try.

2. **Learn from Mistakes:** Each mistake is a lesson in disguise. When you stumble, take a moment to reflect. What went wrong? Why did it go wrong? What could you have done differently? By asking these questions, you turn your mistakes into valuable learning opportunities, each one a stepping stone towards growth.

3. **Persistence and Resilience:** When problems come up, it's essential to keep going. Try not to give up as soon as things get complicated. Try again, try something different, but don't give up. With the ability to get back up after failures and setbacks,

which is called resilience, persistence becomes an unstoppable force.

To demonstrate this, let's consider J.K. Rowling, renowned for her authorship of the Harry Potter series. Before her first book was finally published, she had to deal with many rejections and hard times. At one point, she was a single mom who got help from welfare and struggled to pay the bills. But she didn't let the way things stopped her. Even though she was turned down, she kept writing. In the end, her book was published and it became one of the most popular series in the world. That's how important it is to turn obstacles into stepping stones.

> TURN YOUR PROBLEMS INTO OPPORTUNITIES AND WATCH AS THEY HELP YOU GET WHERE YOU WANT.

In the game of Life, you are the player and hold the controller. Every obstacle is a chance to learn, grow, and move up in your game. So, take the leap, face the challenge, and remember that even if you fall, you haven't lost the game; you've just found a way that doesn't lead to the finish line…yet. And each time you try, you get one step closer to how that works. Turn your problems into opportunities and watch as they help you get where you want.

No good sailor was ever made by a calm sea.

EXERCISE 1:

Turning Problems Into Opportunities

Think back to when you were under pressure or faced a challenge. What was happening?

....
....
....
....
....

What did you do at the time? Now that you've thought about it, how could you have turned that obstacle into a stepping stone? What changes would you make if this happens again? Write a short reflection, and then plan for what to do in similar cases in the future.

....
....
....
....
....

A Critic's Guide to Constructive Feedback

Have you ever been given advice that, at first, hurt, but later turned out to be incredibly valuable? That's constructive feedback which is like a medicine that might taste bitter but ultimately helps you recover and grow stronger.

In a society where views and assessments are rapidly exchanged, it becomes crucial to discern the difference between destructive criticism and constructive feedback. This distinction becomes even more critical as you step into leadership roles where feedback becomes a cornerstone of your growth and development.

Let's dive into how you can embrace and use constructive Feedback to your advantage:

1. **Understanding Constructive Feedback:** Constructive feedback is meant to help you improve. It is specific, actionable, and provided to help you grow. Unlike destructive criticism, which is often vague and discouraging, constructive feedback focuses on your actions and behaviours, not you as a person.
2. **Accepting Feedback:** It's natural to experience a twinge of defensiveness when someone provides feedback. After all, it's human nature to be a little resistant when we hear something challenging our current way of doing things. But remember, constructive feedback isn't about right or wrong; it's about improvement. By viewing feedback as a tool for growth, you can shift your mindset and start accepting Feedback more openly.
3. **Applying Feedback:** Accepting feedback is the first step, but real growth comes from applying it. Reflect on the feedback you've received. What changes can you make? How can you incorporate this feedback into your actions?

Let's illustrate this with a story. Imagine a budding writer who just completed their first short story. Excited and proud, they share it with their mentor. The mentor reads it carefully and then provides Feedback. They highlight the story's strengths but also point out areas for improvement: the plot could be more engaging, the characters could be more developed, and the descriptions could be more vivid.

The writer might initially feel disappointed. But then, they remember that this feedback isn't a personal attack; it's a tool to help them improve. They accept the feedback, reflect on it, and then revise their story, keeping the mentor's comments in mind. The next version of their story is noticeably better, more engaging, and more vivid.

That's the power of constructive feedback. It's not about pointing out flaws but fostering growth, enhancing skills, and pushing you towards betterment. So next time you receive Feedback, remember the young writer. Don't shy away from it; embrace it. See it not as a discouragement but as an opportunity—a critic's guide to your personal improvement.

> IT'S NOT ABOUT POINTING OUT FLAWS BUT FOSTERING GROWTH, ENHANCING SKILLS, AND PUSHING YOU TOWARDS BETTERMENT.

In your journey to becoming young leaders, constructive feedback will be essential. Remember, feedback isn't meant to pull you down; it's there to lift you up, one step at a time. So, equip yourself with the understanding, acceptance, and application of constructive feedback, and prepare to soar to new heights.

Pressure Cooker: How to Keep Your Cool.

If you've ever watched a pressure cooker in action, you'll know it can quickly transform raw ingredients into a flavorful meal. But, as the heat and pressure inside the cooker increase, so does the intensity of the steam that needs to escape. Imagine yourself as that pressure cooker. Life puts us under various pressures and like the cooker, we need ways to release that steam.

1. **Understanding Pressure:** It's important to know that pressure isn't always insufficient. In fact, a certain amount of force can push us towards accomplishing our goals and improving our performance. But when the pressure becomes too much, it can lead to stress and affect our mental health. This is when we need strategies to manage it and keep our cool.
2. **Identifying Your Pressure Points:** Each person experiences pressure differently. What might be a minor inconvenience to one person might feel like a significant stressor to another. This might encompass anything, from delivering public speeches and grappling with stringent deadlines to handling contentious disputes. You can develop strategies to deal with your unique pressure points effectively by identifying your unique pressure points.
3. **Techniques to Keep Your Cool:** Various techniques can help you manage pressure. This can include relaxation techniques like deep breathing and meditation, physical activities like exercise or even a short walk, or cognitive strategies like positive self-talk and reframing your perspective.
4. **Seeking Support:** Remember, you don't have to manage pressure alone. Reach out to trusted friends, family, mentors, or professionals. They can provide advice, a listening ear, or a new perspective.

To explain this, consider the story of a young soccer player. They were an excellent player during practice but felt immense pressure during games, often resulting in mistakes. This was their pressure point—performing in public under scrutiny. They sought help from a coach, who taught them visualization techniques and stress-management strategies. Over time, these techniques helped them achieve better during games and they could enjoy the sport they loved without being overwhelmed by pressure.

The world of entrepreneurship provides numerous examples of young individuals who've faced immense pressure. For instance, consider the story of Ben Pasternak. When he was merely 15, this young lad from Australia left high school behind and embarked on a journey to New York City to bring his innovative app concept to life.

The "Flogg" app was a marketplace for teenagers to buy and sell within their community. Ben showed incredible resilience when facing the immense pressure of building a business while navigating a new city alone. However, like most entrepreneurs, he faced setbacks. Flogg didn't become the success he'd hoped for.

Instead of letting the pressure get to him, Ben learned from the experience and bounced back. He used the lessons learned to co-found another company, "Monkey" which was later acquired by a leading tech company. Ben's journey is a testament to the power of resilience and keeping calm under pressure.

IRRESPECTIVE OF YOUR SITUATION, THE GOAL ISN'T TO EVADE PRESSURE BUT RATHER TO CULTIVATE THE SKILL OF STEERING THROUGH IT.

Always bear in mind, irrespective of your situation, the goal isn't to evade pressure but rather to cultivate the skill of steering through it. It's not about avoiding pressure but learning to navigate it. Sometimes, pressure can even be the catalyst that helps you leap towards your goals, just as the pressure in a cooker transforms raw ingredients into a delightful meal.

 EXERCISE 2:

Pressure Cooker Moments

When did you feel like you were under a lot of pressure? It could be a complex project, a stern test, or a conversation. What did you think?

....
....
....
....
....

How did you react? How did you stay calm? Did it work? Write your thoughts and consider if there's a better way to handle it next time. Also, think of ways to prepare for these situations so you won't be caught off guard.

....
....
....
....
....

Wisdom Wrapping

In life, just like in a pressure cooker, it's essential to have ways to release steam. The strategies that have been mentioned above can be your whistle on the pressure cooker, allowing you to release pressure in a safe and controlled manner. Remember, the goal isn't to sidestep stress but rather to master the art of navigating it. This way, you can continue flourishing and progressing despite the most demanding circumstances.

Embrace the heat, handle the pressure, and trust yourself to transform into something beautiful and strong, just like the pressure-cooked meal. In the end, remember, it's under high pressure that a mere chunk of carbon transforms into a precious diamond.

CHAPTER 5

CHOOSE YOUR ADVENTURE

*L*ife can feel like an uncharted adventure, bringing new choices, challenges, and opportunities each day. The choices we make not only determine the path of our journey but also shape our identity. This chapter, dear young leaders, is designed to help you navigate this intricate maze of decisions that life presents.

We start by discussing 'The Dangerous Allure of the Forbidden Fruit,' a topic often shrouded in silence and misconceptions—peer pressure, especially around drugs and substance abuse. Understanding this challenge is the first step to making informed decisions and safeguarding your health and future.

Next, we'll delve into 'The Decision-Making Map,' a guide to decision-making's vital role in effective leadership. Through this, you'll understand the impact and value of your choices, not just on your life but on those around you as well.

We will end with 'Your Internal GPS: Making Choices that Matter,' where we equip you with practical strategies for making wise and informed decisions. Think of it as calibrating your internal compass to guide you reliably through your journey.

Remember, the choices you make shape your adventure. Let's ensure you're equipped to make the best ones possible. Now, let's dive into the first sub-chapter, 'The Dangerous Allure of the Forbidden Fruit.'

The Dangerous Allure of the Forbidden Fruit

In your journey through adolescence and early adulthood, you'll encounter many tantalizing prospects—the forbidden fruits, so to speak. These might be risk-taking adventures, bending the rules for thrill or status, or succumbing to peer pressure to fit into specific social groups. While some of these experiences may seem exciting and even essential to growing up, it's important to understand the implications of your choices.

One form of the forbidden fruit is risk-taking behaviour, often manifested in adventurous or dangerous activities. For example, you might be tempted to drive at high speeds for the adrenaline rush or to prove your braveness to friends. Or you may consider skipping school or classes to exert your independence. While these acts might give you a momentary thrill or a sense of rebellion, they carry significant risks and potential long-term consequences. They can jeopardize your safety, your education, and your future.

Another form of the forbidden fruit is succumbing to peer pressure to fit in. The yearning for acceptance and belonging within your peer group can wield significant influence. It can make you do things you usually wouldn't do or make decisions against your judgment. Remember, true courage is not merely fulfilling what others expect of you. Rather, it springs from the audacious act of standing by your values and convictions, even if it requires standing apart from the crowd.

A third form of the forbidden fruit can be found in the digital world. With the rise of social media, It's pretty simple to become engrossed in the enticing realm of online challenges that are often dangerous and senseless, just for the sake of likes, shares, or virality. Or you might be tempted to share too much personal information online, lured by the illusion of popularity or the desire for validation.

The allure of these forbidden fruits is indeed strong. But as future leaders, you need to understand the difference between short-term thrill and long-term gain. It's about making wise decisions and prioritizing your safety, well-being, and future.

In the coming sub-chapters, we'll explore how to navigate these complex choices and develop strong decision-making skills. We'll equip you with a 'Decision-Making Map' and guide you to tune into 'Your Internal GPS' to make choices that truly matter.

> BUT AS FUTURE LEADERS, YOU NEED TO UNDERSTAND THE DIFFERENCE BETWEEN SHORT-TERM THRILL AND LONG-TERM GAIN.

Remember, it's your adventure, your life. Don't let the allure of the forbidden fruit steer you off your path. Stand firm, make wise decisions, and be the leader you're meant to be.

 EXERCISE 1:

Navigating the Allure of Forbidden Fruit: Reflect on a moment when you felt pressured to go along with something you weren't comfortable with. What did you do? What did you think? How differently would you respond if you face a similar situation? Write down your thoughts.

....
....
....

The Decision-Making Map

Life is a never-ending series of decisions, isn't it? From the moment we awaken to a new day until we surrender to sleep each night, we're continually confronted with many decisions. Some are seemingly insignificant, like deciding whether to snooze your alarm clock for five more minutes or get up immediately. Others are more substantial, like choosing a college major, a career path, or the values we wish to live by.

Imagine you're standing in front of a vast map, the map of your life. Each decision you make is a step in one direction or another on this map. Your choices can lead you to exciting new territories or a complicated maze. Making the right decisions can set you on a path that aligns with your values and goals, leading you toward a fulfilling and successful life.

> YOUR CHOICES CAN LEAD YOU TO EXCITING NEW TERRITORIES OR A COMPLICATED MAZE.

So, what influences our decisions? As a teen or a young adult, you may notice three significant influencers: the opinions of others (especially peers), your emotions, and your values and beliefs. Each has its role and it's crucial to strike a balance between them. Imagine a situation: You've been offered a part in the school play, but your friends don't think it's cool. You love acting, but you also want to maintain your friend's opinion of you here, the influence of peers conflicts with your passion and belief in your acting skills.

How do we navigate such situations? Well, here are a few steps to follow:

1. **Assess the Situation:** Take a step back and examine the bigger picture. What are the possible outcomes? What's at stake?
2. **Consider Your Values:** What do you believe in? What's important to you? If you value creativity and self-expression, being part of the play aligns with these values.
3. **Tune Into Your Feelings:** How does the thought of accepting or declining the role make you feel? Remember, your emotions are valid and can provide valuable insights.
4. **Seek Advice:** Reach out to a trusted adult, a mentor, or a coach. They can provide a different perspective and some wise advice.
5. **Make a Decision:** After considering all these aspects, make a well-informed decision. Trust in your ability to make sound choices.

Remember, as a young leader, it's not always about making the popular decision but about making the decision that aligns with your values and helps you grow. This is what the 'Decision-Making Map' is all about. So, the next time you're faced with a tough decision, take out your map and chart your course!

 EXERCISE 2:

Your Decision-Making Map: Think about a recent significant decision. What values, principles, or aspects of self-awareness guided you in making that decision? Were you happy with the outcome? If not, how could you better use your Internal GPS in the future?

....
....
....
....
....

Your Internal GPS: Making Choices that Matter

Have you ever used a GPS while travelling or hiking? It's an incredibly handy device, isn't it? You feed it the destination and it guides you on the most efficient route, informs you of upcoming turns, alerts you if you're going off track, and even helps you reorient yourself if you veer off the right path. Well, wouldn't it be wonderful to have a GPS for life decisions?

For example, if you value honesty, you'll feel a sense of pride when you stand up for the truth, even when it's tough to do so.

Your principles are the road rules that guide your journey. They are the codes of conduct you set for yourself, like always treating others with kindness or standing up for what you believe in. Following these principles, even when the going gets tough, ensures you stay true to yourself and maintain your integrity.

And finally, self-awareness is like the satellite that tracks where you currently are. It's about understanding your emotions, strengths, weaknesses, and areas of growth. Self-awareness lets you know when you're off-track and helps you get back on course. It's the tool that enables you to reflect, learn, and grow from every decision.

Take the story of Aisha, a high school student passionate about protecting the environment. Aisha's values included sustainability and community welfare. She had principles of honesty, hard work, and integrity. She was also self-aware, understanding her strengths, such as her leadership abilities and persuasion skills, and her areas of growth, such as her fear of public speaking.

One day, her school decided to organize a massive event, and they planned to use disposable plastic cutlery for convenience. Aisha was in a dilemma. She could keep quiet, avoid the fear of public speaking, and let the event proceed as planned, or she could speak up, face her fear, and advocate for more sustainable options.

She consulted her Internal GPS. Her values of sustainability and community welfare urged her to take a stand. Her principles reminded her of the importance of honesty and integrity, pushing her to voice her concerns despite the discomfort. Her self-awareness made her recognize her fear of public speaking as an opportunity for growth.

Aisha chose to speak up. She presented her arguments and alternative solutions to the event committee, facing her fear of public speaking. Impressed by her passion and well-reasoned arguments, the committee decided to switch to reusable cutlery for the event.

Aisha's decision led to a more sustainable event and helped her overcome her fear of public speaking. She realized that her Internal GPS had guided her well. By aligning her decision with her values and principles and using her self-awareness, Aisha made a choice that positively impacted her school community and her personal growth.

This story underlines the power of using your Internal GPS in decision-making. Like Aisha, your values, principles, and self-awareness can guide you in making choices that matter and contribute positively to your personal journey and the world around you. So, take control of your preferences. Navigate wisely, dear young leader, and your rewarding adventure awaits!

> YOUR VALUES ARE YOUR DESTINATION—THE BIG-PICTURE GOALS OF WHAT YOU WANT YOUR LIFE TO STAND FOR.

Let me introduce you to your Internal GPS—your values, principles, and self-awareness. This GPS may not speak in a robotic voice, but it has a language of its own—a language of feelings, intuition, and reflection. It's about learning to listen and trust yourself.

Your values are your destination—the big-picture goals of what you want your life to stand for. When you align your decisions with your core values, you experience a deeper sense of gratification and contentment.

 EXERCISE 3:

Fine-tuning Your Internal GPS: Reflect on your core values and principles. List them down. Now, consider your areas of strength and areas of growth. How can you use this self-awareness to guide your future decisions? Create an action plan for fine-tuning your Internal GPS.

....
....
....
....
....

Remember to revisit these exercises occasionally as you grow and evolve. Your reflections may change, and that's perfectly okay. That's a sign of growth. Good luck on your journey, young leader!

Wisdom Wrapping

Your Internal GPS won't be perfect, and that's okay. Sometimes, you may take wrong turns or miss the signs, but every decision, right or wrong, offers an opportunity for growth and learning. Mistakes are a part of life and are often our greatest teachers. What's important is to keep learning, growing, and striving to make choices that align with your values and principles.

So, the next time you're faced with a decision, take a moment to consult your Internal GPS. Listen to your feelings, consider your values, and apply your principles. And remember, it's not just about the destination but the journey. Every decision you make shapes this journey, contributing to the person you are becoming and the legacy you will leave behind. Choose wisely, young leader. Your adventure awaits!

CHAPTER 6

THE POWER OF THE SPOKEN WORD

*F*rom the ancient art of storytelling around a crackling fire to our modern world of TED talks and viral social media posts, the power of the spoken word remains an indomitable force. It bridges distances, closes gaps, and forges connections across continents and cultures. At its best, it's a superpower that can motivate, inspire, and lead change. At its worst, it's a weapon that can divide, hurt, and cause chaos. The fine line between the two is drawn by effective communication and understanding the weight and worth of our words.

This chapter will guide our young leaders on how to wield this power responsibly, with purpose and precision. We will delve into the essentials of effective communication, the delicate art of weaving relationships through conversations, and the subtle science of influencing without authority. It's not just about talking but about truly communicating, where the real victory lies not in being heard but in being understood. From group discussions at school to negotiations in the boardroom, the skills honed in this chapter will be invaluable in your leadership arsenal. Let's embark on this journey to unlock the magic and power of the spoken word.

The ABCs of Effective Communication

Looking back at my decade-long journey of mentoring young adults and teens, I realize that effective communication is one of the most powerful tools I've imparted to them. This isn't about using fancy words or mastering public speaking, it's about understanding the ABCs of communication. I call them the 'building blocks' of any fruitful conversation: attention, bridge, and clarity.

Attention: Be present, attentive, and observant in your communication. Listen more than you speak, and when you do speak, ensure your words are adding value to the conversation. Attention to the other person's words, tone, body language, and cues will help you understand them better.

Bridge: Bridge any gaps in communication by understanding the perspectives of others and then bridging the differences through dialogue. Empathy, understanding, and respecting each other's viewpoints are integral to this process.

Clarity: Be clear and concise in your communication. Ambiguity often leads to misunderstanding and conflicts. So, ensure your thoughts, ideas, and intentions are communicated clearly and correctly.

Over the years, I've seen these simple yet profound principles transform how my mentees interact with their peers, teachers, and family. Anxious students became confident presenters, introverted individuals actively participated in group discussions, and misfits became leaders. These transformations were not overnight miracles; they were the results of consistent efforts in understanding and applying these ABCs of communication.

In the age of smartphones and social media, communication has become faster and easier. However, effective communication, which brings people together and fosters understanding, respect, and cooperation, has become even more crucial. As young leaders, mastering this skill will enable you to inspire others, lead effectively, and make a real difference in your world.

> AS YOUNG LEADERS, MASTERING THIS SKILL WILL ENABLE YOU TO INSPIRE OTHERS, LEAD EFFECTIVELY, AND MAKE A REAL DIFFERENCE IN YOUR WORLD.

So, take a moment to reflect on your own communication style. How often do you truly pay attention to the person you're communicating with? Do you try to bridge the gap and understand others' perspectives? Is your message clear and concise? Remember, understanding and improving the ABCs of your communication will make you a better speaker, listener, understanding person, and ultimately, a better leader.

 EXERCISE 1:
Reflect on Your Conversations

Reflect on a meaningful conversation you had recently. It could be with a friend, family member, or anyone else.

- What made this conversation meaningful to you?

....

- What did you learn from it?

....

- How can you incorporate this into your future discussions?

....

Relationship Weaving: Threads of Conversation

In the vast tapestry of our lives, each relationship is a unique thread, interwoven with the others, forming an intricate design. The key to weaving this relationship tapestry is through lines of conversation—these dynamic exchanges that form the bonds that connect us.

As young adults and teens, you are at a stage where you are constantly building and nurturing relationships. For some, navigating the intricacies of relationships might come effortlessly, while others may grapple with it. Nevertheless, cultivating relationships. This delightful process of relationship weaving is a competency that can be developed and refined over time. In this endeavour, your most influential instrument is undoubtedly the power of conversation.

Conversation is not just about talking. It's about listening, understanding, sharing, connecting, and, sometimes, about being comfortable in silence. It's about being genuine in your interactions, open and vulnerable, and respecting the other person's boundaries. It's about acknowledging differences and celebrating commonalities. It's about disagreements and reconciliations. It's not only about expressing your thoughts and feelings but also about understanding and validating the thoughts and feelings of the other person.

Think about the conversations you've had recently. Did they feel like genuine exchanges or mere transactions? Did you feel connected to the other person or did it feel like you were talking at cross purposes?

In the context of leadership, effective conversations can inspire and motivate, resolve conflicts, build trust, and foster collaboration. As young leaders, having effective discussions is a crucial skill that can help you build strong, positive relationships with your team members, peers, and seniors.

To build your skill in relationship weaving, start paying conscious attention to your conversations. Start small with your daily interactions. Listen more attentively. Try to understand the other person's perspective. Be genuine in your responses. Over time, you will notice a shift in the quality of your conversations and relationships. Remember, every conversation is an opportunity to learn, connect, and build relationships.

So, the next time you're conversing, ask yourself, "How can I weave this thread more effectively?" The answer might surprise you.

The Subtle Art of Influencing Without Authority

Have you ever found yourself in a situation where you needed to get something done but didn't have the direct authority to make it happen? You are not alone as this is a common situation, especially for young leaders who might not hold official positions of power. The question then arises, how do you influence decisions and inspire action without wielding authority? Welcome to the subtle art of influencing without authority.

Let me share a story with you. As a teenager, I had an idea for a community cleanup event in my neighbourhood. I wasn't the head of the community council or an influential figure; I was merely a teenager with a vision. But with a clear goal in mind and a burning passion, I set out to convince my community to come together for this cause.

First, I had to get the word out about my idea and so, I started by talking to my neighbours. I listened to their concerns and suggestions, engaged with them genuinely, and demonstrated my commitment to the idea. I wasn't ordering people around; instead, I was inviting them to be part of a collective solution. Gradually, the idea gained traction. I remember the day over fifty people from my neighbourhood came together to clean our local park. That day, I learned a valuable lesson about the power of influence without authority.

Influence without authority doesn't mean being manipulative or deceiving. It's about building trust, fostering relationships, demonstrating competence, and showing that you care about the team's success as much as your own. It's about leading through example, persuasion, and negotiation, rather than directives. In a world that often equates leadership with authority, it's essential to understand that real influence transcends official roles or titles.

> IT'S ABOUT BUILDING TRUST, FOSTERING RELATIONSHIPS, DEMONSTRATING COMPETENCE, AND SHOWING THAT YOU CARE ABOUT THE TEAM'S SUCCESS AS MUCH AS YOUR OWN.

True leaders inspire others to act not because they are told to but because they genuinely want to. They influence not through command but through inspiration, not by mandate but by example. They create an environment where everyone feels empowered to contribute, every idea is valued, and everyone is motivated to work towards a shared goal.

Whether you're trying to organize a school event, convince your friends to join a cause, or work on a team project, the ability to influence without authority can be a powerful tool in your leadership toolbox.

 EXERCISE 2:

Your Influencing Strategy

Think about a time you could influence a decision or a person without formal authority.

- What tactics did you use?

....
....
....

- How did the person respond?

....
....
....

- What would you do differently next time?

....
....
....

The Leadership Blueprint

 EXERCISE 3:

Practicing Influence Without Authority

For this exercise, think about a goal you have that requires the cooperation of others, but you don't have direct authority over them.

- What strategies can you use to gain their support?

....
....
....

- How will you communicate your vision to them?

....
....
....

- What possible obstacles might you face and how could you overcome them?

....
....
....

Take some time to ponder over these questions and jot down your thoughts. Remember, there's no 'right' answer. The goal is to encourage introspection and foster your understanding of the concepts discussed in this chapter. These exercises should serve as a guide that helps you apply what you've learned in your own life.

Wisdom Wrapping

Ultimately, leadership is less about the power to command and more about the ability to inspire. It's about making others feel valued, empowered, and inspired to give their best. So, remember, even if you don't hold an official position of power, you can still be a leader. The key is to learn and master the subtle art of influencing without authority.

CHAPTER 7

THE ART OF EMPATHY

*E*mpathy—a simple word, yet filled with profound significance. It's a silent thread that weaves through the fabric of our society, binding us together. As human beings, we're inherently social creatures. We thrive on connection, understanding, and shared experiences. And it is empathy that creates this bridge between us. Empathy equips us to perceive the world from another's vantage point, engage in their joyous moments, comprehend their struggles, and navigate life's labyrinth.

In this chapter, we'll embark on a voyage to understand empathy and its vital role. We'll delve into its impact on our relationships and how it shapes our interactions. We'll explore how we can express empathy and how, through this expression, we can forge deeper connections, build stronger relationships, and facilitate a more understanding and compassionate society.

Moreover, we'll understand the power of empathy in conflict resolution. Disagreements and conflicts are a part of life but how we navigate them shapes our relationships. With empathy, we can transform these interactions, turning potential battlegrounds into platforms for understanding and mutual respect.

Finally, we'll also explore the role of empathy in fostering inclusivity because empathy isn't just about understanding different perspectives; it's about valuing them. It's about acknowledging the beauty of diversity and using it as a tool to promote inclusivity and unity.

As we delve deeper into this chapter, I encourage you to unlock your hearts and minds, plunge into the profound realm of empathy, and uncover its transformative power on your relationships, leadership prowess, and, ultimately, your life.

Understanding and Expressing Empathy

Imagine walking along the seashore, the waves lapping at your feet, the sand crunching under your steps. Suddenly, you spot someone sitting alone in the distance, their shoulders drooping, their head bowed. You can't hear their thoughts or feel their heartache, but the solitude surrounding them paints a picture of melancholy. This, dear readers, is the first step towards understanding empathy. It's in that simple recognition, acknowledging another's emotional state, even without words.

Empathy, however, isn't just about identifying emotions. It's also about expressing your understanding. Imagine you choose to approach this person on the beach. You don't rush in with solutions or try to brighten their day with forced positivity. Instead, you sit silently beside them, mirroring their quiet contemplation. This quiet companionship, this small but significant act communicates much more than words ever could.

It silently echoes, "I acknowledge your feelings. You're not alone." This, dear emerging leaders, captures the heart of what it means to express empathy.

Empathy is pivotal in our interactions, providing the building blocks for meaningful connections. It allows us to truly listen, not just to the words someone says but to the unspoken feelings hidden behind them. As teenagers and young adults, you're exposed to a world brimming with diverse perspectives and experiences. Empathy equips you with the ability to navigate this diversity, fostering a sense of understanding and mutual respect.

> EMPATHY IS PIVOTAL IN OUR INTERACTIONS, PROVIDING THE BUILDING BLOCKS FOR MEANINGFUL CONNECTIONS.

Moreover, empathy fosters resilience. Empathizing with others makes you more adept at handling your emotions. You realize that everyone, including you, goes through tough times. You learn that feeling sad, angry, or scared is okay. You understand that emotions aren't signs of weakness but symbols of our shared human experience.

Now, let's be clear; empathy doesn't mean you have to agree with everyone's feelings or actions. Rather, it's about understanding their viewpoint and acknowledging their emotions. It's also about validating their experiences, even if they differ from your own.

During one of my early coaching sessions with a group of teens, I remember conducting an exercise where each participant had to share a personal story and others had to listen empathetically. The results were astounding. The young leaders began to understand their peers better and expressed their feelings more openly. They realized that empathy wasn't just about understanding others but also about understanding and expressing their own emotions.

As we navigate this chapter, I aim to furnish you with the resources to grasp and express empathy more effectively. Moving ahead, we'll delve into empathy's role in mediating conflicts and its contribution towards fostering inclusivity and comprehension.

 WORKSHEET 1:

Understanding and Expressing Empathy

1. Reflect on a time when you felt truly understood by someone. How did they demonstrate empathy? What impact did it have on you? Write down your thoughts.

....
....
....
....

2. Choose a person in your life—a friend, family member, teacher or anyone else. Try to put yourself in their shoes for a day. Write down how you think they might feel and why.

....
....
....
....

The Role of Empathy in Conflict Resolution

When you hear the word "conflict," what springs to mind? Is it an argument? A fight? A disagreement? Well, you're not entirely wrong. While conflict might stir unease within us, it's an inherent aspect of human interactions and doesn't always signify a setback. In fact, when handled correctly, conflict can often lead to growth, learning, and deeper understanding.

But here's the key to making that positive shift—empathy.

Empathy plays a crucial role in conflict resolution. It enables us to grasp the other individual's perspective, perceive the world from their standpoint, and recognize their sentiments and emotions. It's an essential skill for effective leaders and a skill you can develop with practice.

Consider this scenario momentarily: you're at school, embroiled in a passionate discussion with a classmate over a group assignment. Your classmate believes your group should take one approach, but you disagree, advocating for another method. Tempers flare, words are exchanged, and tension fills the air. At that moment, it's so easy to get caught up in the heat of the conflict, focusing only on your viewpoint and disregarding your classmate's perspective.

However, this is exactly when empathy can act as your guiding star. You can diffuse the situation by taking a step back, breathing, and trying to understand your classmate's viewpoint.

As an alternative to becoming defensive, you might respond, "I can understand your perspective and why you believe that method could be effective. Here's why I have a different perspective..." In this manner, you're not disregarding their ideas but rather initiating a dialogue where both individuals can learn and evolve from the conflict.

Remember here that empathy in conflict resolution isn't about "winning" an argument. It's about reaching an understanding, a compromise that respects everyone's perspectives. It's about turning that heated disagreement into an opportunity for growth, learning, and connection.

Conflicts can be challenging and uncomfortable, but they are also opportunities. Instances of conflict are chances to learn, develop, comprehend, and express empathy.

> INSTANCES OF CONFLICT ARE CHANCES TO LEARN, DEVELOP, COMPREHEND, AND EXPRESS EMPATHY.

Therefore, the next time you find yourself in a disagreement, take a moment, breathe, and attempt to perceive the situation from the other person's viewpoint. Empathy is critical to fostering a more harmonious, understanding, and collaborative environment, which is indeed a skill worth honing.

 WORKSHEET 2:

The Role of Empathy in Conflict Resolution

1. Reflect on a conflict or disagreement you had recently. Try to understand the other person's perspective and write down what you think they felt and why.

....
....
....
....

2. Had you approached the situation with more empathy, how different would it have been? Write down some actions you could have taken to demonstrate empathy during the disagreement.

....
....

The Inclusive Leader's Handbook

In the vast tapestry of humanity, there is a multitude of colours, each unique, each vibrant, and each contributing to the overall beauty of the piece. As young leaders, one of the most valuable skills you can develop is creating an environment where every thread, every colour, and every individual feels valued and included.

But what does inclusivity truly mean? It goes beyond mere tolerance or acceptance. Inclusivity is valuing diversity and making conscious efforts to include everyone, regardless of their background, beliefs, abilities, or experiences. It's about fostering a space where everyone feels comfortable expressing themselves authentically, where everyone feels heard, and where everyone's input is valued.

Believe it or not, the key to promoting inclusivity circles back to our earlier discussion about empathy. When you cultivate the capacity to share the emotions of others, envision the world through their lens, and recognize and respect their experiences, you're already taking strides towards evolving into a more inclusive leader.

Luis, who, despite being only in his early twenties, has risen to the position of team leader in a small but ambitious startup. The "Green Innovations" startup focuses on developing eco-friendly solutions for everyday problems.

Luis leads a diverse team of talented individuals from various cultural backgrounds. He values each member's perspective and ensures everyone feels heard and appreciated. One day, Luis proposes a new project for the team. Still, during the brainstorming session, he notices a team member, Lin, who usually contributes brilliant ideas, has been unusually silent.

Wanting to ensure Lin feels included, Luis gently prompts her to share her thoughts. Lin explains that while she loves the project's premise, she feels the design needs to consider users from something other than her cultural background. Luis listens attentively, thanks Lin for her valuable perspective, and invites her to help refine the design to become more inclusive.

In this instance, Luis exercised empathy to create an inclusive environment. He noticed when a team member seemed disengaged and made an effort to understand her perspective. He made Lin feel valued and included and improved the project by ensuring it catered to a wider audience.

Inclusive leadership, such as Luis', recognizes and values each individual's perspectives. It's about ensuring everyone feels seen, heard, and appreciated, regardless of their cultural background or personal experiences.

By fostering a culture of inclusivity, you can drive creativity, innovation, and success in whatever venture you undertake. And most importantly, you can create a space where everyone feels valued and respected, enhancing team collaboration and unity.

As a young leader, you can create such an environment in your school, community, or future workplace. The first step? Exercising empathy.

Being an inclusive leader also means being aware of and challenging your biases. We all have preferences, but the difference lies in whether we let them cloud our judgment or whether we actively work against them. To be inclusive, we must constantly question our biases, seek to understand others, and appreciate their unique contributions.

> BUT THE DIFFERENCE LIES IN WHETHER WE LET THEM CLOUD OUR JUDGMENT OR WHETHER WE ACTIVELY WORK AGAINST THEM.

Inclusivity is a journey, not a destination. It requires constant learning, unlearning, and relearning. But the effort is worth it. An inclusive environment breeds creativity, innovation, and collaboration. It encourages individuals to present their authentic selves in discussions, leading to more comprehensive and vigorous conversations that culminate in improved outcomes.

 WORKSHEET 3:
The Inclusive Leader's Handbook

1. Think of a situation where you were in a group with diverse members. Did you find including everyone in the discussion or decision-making process challenging? How could you have done better? Jot down your reflections.

....
....
....

2. Imagine you are leading a diverse team. What steps would you take to ensure all team members feel heard, understood, and valued? Draft an action plan.

....
....
....
....

Remember, these exercises are meant to encourage reflection and self-awareness. Be honest with yourself; there are no right or wrong answers. The key is to learn and grow from each experience.

Wisdom Wrapping

As young leaders, your task is to promote inclusivity in your circles. Whether in your school, community, or future workplaces, strive to create environments where everyone feels included. Understand that your actions and words can be bridges of understanding or barriers to division. Choose to be a bridge. Remember, inclusivity begins with 'I.'

So let's start today. Let's start now. Let's weave a tapestry that is as diverse and beautiful as our world. Because, in the end, we're all threads in the same tapestry, interconnected and interdependent. And together, we can create a masterpiece.

And on this note, we wrap up our discussion on empathy and its role in our lives as young leaders. We've explored the heart from different angles, understood its importance, and seen how it can make us better leaders. But remember…

CHAPTER 8

CHANGE MAKERS AMONG US

*I*n the grand theater of life, there are many performers. Among these, a select few stand out, their performances etching indelible marks in the sands of time. These are the young leaders, the visionaries, the change-makers. Regardless of their age or circumstances, they have stepped forward, accepted the mantle of responsibility, and committed themselves to the cause of positive change. This chapter, dear young leaders, is a tribute to them and a guide for you - it's about acknowledging the potential you hold to be among these change-makers and equipping you with the practical wisdom to put theory into action.

Young leaders are like hidden gems, their brilliance often concealed under the veneer of youth and inexperience. Yet, once discovered and polished, their radiance can outshine even the most dazzling stars. These leaders, many of whom are scarcely older than you, create a ripple of change across the globe, challenge the status quo, and inspire others to follow suit.

Creating an impact doesn't require grand gestures or colossal resources; sometimes, the smallest pebble causes the most significant ripple. The effect can begin in your backyard, school, and community. It's about identifying an issue that resonates with you and taking the first step to address it, no matter how small. It's about understanding that every action, and every decision, contributes to the broader tapestry of societal change.

Leadership isn't merely about inspiring speeches and grandiose plans; it's as much about action as it is about ideation. This chapter will take you further, from understanding leadership theories to implementing them. By learning from the young leaders who have walked this path before and understanding the practical aspects of leading change, you'll be better equipped to embrace the challenges and opportunities that leadership brings. As you continue to navigate your leadership path, keep in mind: leadership is not a destination; it's a journey, and every step you take, no matter how small, counts.

Young Leaders: The World's Hidden Gems

Some young leaders are often overlooked in every corner of our world - the unsung heroes and the quiet revolutionaries. These are the world's hidden gems, poised to sparkle and illuminate the world with their passion, potential, and tenacity. Let's explore how these young leaders can transform not solely their own lives, but also the lives of those around them and, indeed, the world at large.

Consider the narrative about Lisa, a young trailblazer who, at the young age of 14, took it upon herself to address the issue of literacy in her community. She had observed that many children in her neighbourhood didn't have access to books and educational resources, and she was determined to change that. She didn't wait for someone else to step up or for the ideal circumstances to arrive. She had an idea, believed in it, and took action. She established a community library in her backyard using her saved pocket money and rallying support from her friends, family, and neighbours. She stocked it with donated books, ran reading sessions, and set up a book-lending system. Despite being young, Lisa's proactive steps led to real, tangible change in her community, igniting a love for reading among many children.

And then there's Jamal, a high school student passionate about environmental conservation. Disturbed by the litter problem in his local park, he began organizing weekly cleanup drives. Initially, he started this journey alone, but his commitment and the visible transformation of the garden inspired others. Soon, his solo efforts transformed into a community project, drawing individuals from all age groups. His leadership shone through his actions, proving that age does not restrict one's capability to inspire and enact change.

In another part of the world, there's Meena, a 16-year-old tech wizard. She noticed that many elderly people in her community struggled with using technology, which became especially problematic during the pandemic when digital literacy was crucial. Harnessing her skills, she developed simple guides and started free classes to teach the elderly about smartphones, social media, online safety, and more. This bridged the generational and digital gap and fostered new connections in her community.

These young leaders, Lisa, Jamal, and Meena, should have addressed the issues they saw before perfect conditions or for someone else to address the problems they saw. They did not let their age, lack of resources, or fear of failure deter them.

They believed in their ability to create a difference and acted upon it.In my years guiding young leaders, I have seen countless stories of courage, ingenuity, and relentless pursuit of improvement. And each tale reassures me that leadership is not bound by age or experience. Leadership is a mindset, a willingness to step up, take responsibility, and effect change.

So, to all the young leaders out there - remember, you are not just the leaders of tomorrow; you are the change-makers of today. **You don't need a formal title or a specific role to lead.** All you need is a cause you're passionate about and the resolve to act on it. Even the seemingly minor actions you take, regardless of how insignificant they may appear, can have a ripple effect, creating waves of change that can transform your community and even the world. As we delve further into this chapter, let's look at how you can make this ripple effect in your neighbourhood.

> YOU DON'T NEED A FORMAL TITLE OR A SPECIFIC ROLE TO LEAD.

All you need is a cause you're passionate about and the resolve to act on it. Even the seemingly minor actions you take, regardless of how insignificant they may appear, can have a ripple effect, creating waves of change that can transform your community and even the world. As we delve further into this chapter, let's look at how you can make this ripple effect in your neighbourhood.

EXERCISE 1:

Your Leadership Vision Reflect on your personal leadership vision. What kind of leader do you want to become? How do you envision creating an impact in your community? Write a short essay about your vision and the necessary steps.

....
....
....
....

The Ripple Effect: Creating Impact Close to Home

Can you recall the last instance where you gently dropped a small stone into a pond? How the initial splash was quickly followed by expanding circles, or ripples, that travelled far and wide? You see, much like that humble pebble, you too can create ripples of impact starting in your backyard and your community.

It's natural to aspire to make profound and sweeping changes, to want to tackle world hunger or fight climate change. While these goals are noble and important, consider the power of smaller, local actions. Why? Well, because these local actions are the stepping stones to broader change. They are your training ground.

Take, for instance, David, a young leader I met a few years back. David lived in a small town with a population barely exceeding a thousand. There, he noticed that many of his peers were struggling with mental health issues, but very few resources were available to help them.

Rather than sitting back and hoping for others to intervene, David decided to take the reins himself.

He organized a small group of like-minded individuals and established a peer support network in his school. They gathered every week, cultivating a sanctuary where students could express their emotions and share their personal journeys. The initiative started small but gradually grew as more students joined every week. And while David's ambition didn't solve the global mental health crisis, it made a significant difference in his community.

In another instance, Sarah, a vibrant young leader from a middle school, was concerned about the amount of food waste at her school cafeteria. Instead of simply accepting this as an unchangeable reality, she resolved to instigate a change. Sarah initiated a composting program at her school, converting food waste into nutrient-rich compost for the school's garden. Not only did Sarah reduce food waste, but she also enriched the soil and created an opportunity for her peers to learn about sustainability.

In both examples, David and Sarah started with a concern or issue which was close to their heart. They didn't have the resources to make global changes. Still, they took action where they were and with what they had, creating a ripple effect in their communities. The stories of David and Sarah are not unique. Countless young leaders are around you, taking small steps that create substantial local impact. Their actions are like pebbles thrown into a pond, causing ripples of change to radiate outwards. You, too, can make such ripples. Remember, it starts small, right where you are, right at home.

Making an impact isn't about the grandeur of your action but the intention and the effort you put into it. Whether planting a tree in your backyard, tutoring a peer in a difficult subject, or initiating a recycling program in your school, every small act counts.

Being a young leader and change-maker doesn't necessarily mean standing on a global stage. It means making a difference in your unique way right where you are. And as these ripples of your actions expand, they collide with those of others, leading to a wave of change that can reach further than you might ever have imagined.

Remember, a ripple effect begins with a single action. So, what will be your pebble? How will you start your ripple effect in your community? Embrace your potential, take that first step, and see how far your ripples can travel. The power to craft the change you aspire to see is entirely within your grasp. So, start right here, right now. Step into your destiny as the change-maker you were destined to be. Your journey begins with a single step. Embrace it.

> A RIPPLE EFFECT BEGINS WITH A SINGLE ACTION. SO, WHAT WILL BE YOUR PEBBLE?

Your leadership journey is just beginning and the world awaits your influence. The stories in this chapter inspire you and show you that even the smallest actions can have a profound impact. So, as we venture into the final part of this chapter, let's explore some practical tips for putting your leadership skills into action. You are a hidden gem; it's time to shine and make a difference, starting close to home.

 EXERCISE 2:

Identify a Community Issue: Think about a problem in your community or school that you would like to address. Write it down and list why this issue is important and how it affects you and those around you.

....
....
....
....
....
....
....
....

EXERCISE 3:

Create an Action Plan: Based on the issue you identified in Exercise 2, devise a practical action plan. What steps can you take to make a difference? Who might you need to involve? What resources will you require? Sketch out a roadmap for change.

....
....
....
....
....
....
....

Leadership Lab: Putting Theory Into Practice

With every chapter of this book, we've been assembling the toolkit of a true leader: a growth mindset, resilience, decision-making skills, effective communication, empathy, and the drive to make a change. But to truly step into your leadership potential, more than the tools are needed. It's time to apply what we've learned.

This section is about transforming the theory into practice—entering our leadership laboratory, so to speak.

Let's begin by stating a crucial fact. Leadership is not a title; it's a series of actions. It's about showing up, day after day, ready to make a difference. It's about staying true to your values, even when the going gets tough. And it's about constantly seeking opportunities for growth and development, both for yourself and those around you.

In the business world, they often use "on-the-job training." It means learning by doing rather than just studying a subject. Leadership, too, requires this hands-on approach. You can read a thousand books about leadership, but the theory remains abstract until you start practising the principles.

Remember Sophia, our aspiring young writer? She didn't just study literature and writing techniques—she actively started writing her book. And David didn't just sympathize with his fellow students—he put his empathy into action and formed a support group. They brought theory to life by putting their knowledge into practice.

The first step towards becoming a practical leader is identifying opportunities where you can apply your leadership skills. Look around you. What are the issues that bother you in your community? What transformations would you like to witness in your school? Start small. Remember, you aren't expected to revolutionize the world in a day. Begin with what's within your reach and gradually expand your influence.

The second step is to approach these challenges with the tools you've acquired. When faced with a conflict, can you resolve it with empathy and effective communication? Can you tap into your resilience to bounce back when you're under stress? And when you're faced with a tough decision, can you make a choice that aligns with your values?

> THE MOST IMPORTANT PART IS THAT YOU TAKE SOMETHING AWAY FROM THESE EXPERIENCES AND KEEP GETTING BETTER.

The final step is to think about what you did and learn from what happened. Leadership is a journey, not a destination. You'll stumble, you'll fall, and that's okay. The most important part is that you take something away from these experiences and keep getting better.

 EXERCISE 4:

Reflective Journal: At the end of each week, take some time to reflect on your experiences. Did you face any challenges? How did you overcome them? What did you learn from these experiences? Journaling your adventures can be a powerful way to learn from your actions and keep track of your growth.

....
....
....

Remember, the aim of these exercises is to move from thinking about leadership to practising it. The experiences and lessons you gain through these exercises will be invaluable in your journey to becoming a change-maker.

Wisdom Wrapping

Welcome to your leadership lab. This is where the rubber meets the road. This is where you begin to shape your world. The path is yours to carve. So, lace up your shoes and take that first step. Be the leader you know you can be. The world is waiting.

CHAPTER 9
UNLEASHING YOUR INNER DA VINCI

*C*reativity and innovation are often thrown around in business and leadership, but what do they mean for a young leader like you? This chapter seeks to answer that question and guide you on a journey to unleash your inner Leonardo Da Vinci. We will discover the power of blending creativity and innovation in leadership, how to foster innovative thinking, and how to turn your most extravagant daydreams into reality.

Leonardo da Vinci, the Italian polymath from the Renaissance period, was a beacon of creativity and innovation. His boundless curiosity and relentless inventiveness continue to inspire us. He was an artist, an inventor, a scientist, a mathematician, and so much more. But the most vital lesson we can learn from Da Vinci is his ability to think differently, question the status quo, and continuously push the boundaries of what was deemed possible. As young leaders, you are in a unique position to do the same.

Just like Da Vinci's palette had a range of colours, each adding its unique touch to his masterpieces, your leadership palette comprises various skills and qualities. Among them, creativity and innovation hold a unique place. They are the splash of colour that can turn a good leader into an extraordinary one. They allow you to see possibilities where others see problems and turn ideas into actions.

So, are you ready to embark on this exciting journey to discover and ignite your creative and innovative spark? Let's dive in, starting with understanding how creativity and innovation blend into the art and science of leadership.

The Leadership Palette: Blending Creativity and Innovation

Consider leadership as a garden. Creativity is the seed of unique ideas and innovation is the water and sunlight that helps these seeds grow and bear fruits. Without creativity, there would be no seed to plant and without innovation, the seed would remain just a seed, never growing or developing. Creativity and innovation create a beautiful, thriving garden—your leadership style. As we venture further into this chapter, envision yourself as a gardener, prepared to sow the seeds of your ideas and nurture them with innovative thinking until they bloom into reality.

As an artist mixes colours on their palette to create a magnificent painting, a leader blends various skills to craft effective leadership. Two critical components of this leadership palette are creativity and innovation. But what do these terms truly mean and how do they apply to you, a young leader?

> AS AN ARTIST MIXES COLOURS ON THEIR PALETTE TO CREATE A MAGNIFICENT PAINTING, A LEADER BLENDS VARIOUS SKILLS TO CRAFT EFFECTIVE LEADERSHIP.

Creativity is all about generating new and original ideas. It's about thinking outside the box and seeing connections others may not see. It's about being bold enough to challenge the status quo and envision new possibilities. Creativity helps you approach problems from different angles as a leader, leading to more diverse and potentially effective solutions.

Innovation, on the other hand, takes creativity a step further. It's about implementing and transforming these creative ideas into tangible outcomes that lead to progress. As a leader, innovating means taking risks, trying new things, and continuously improving. It's about turning that light bulb moment into a shining beacon of change.

So, why are creativity and innovation vital in leadership, especially for young leaders such as yourself? The answer lies in the rapidly changing world we live in. Today's problems are becoming increasingly complex and multifaceted. Traditional methods and solutions may only sometimes work. Here is where creativity and new ideas can help. They enable us to break free from conventional thinking, explore new avenues, and generate novel solutions.

The world needs more creative and innovative leaders—leaders who can paint a vivid picture of the future, leaders who can bring this vision to life. As we progress through this chapter, we'll dive deeper into how to nurture your innovative mindset and turn your unique ideas into tangible realities. But remember, like every artist, you have your individual style. So, as we explore further, remember there is no one-size-fits-all approach. It's about finding your unique blend on the leadership palette.

EXERCISE 1:

Discovering Your Creativity

Think about a problem you've encountered recently. This could range from a straightforward issue like organizing your study space to a more intricate community-level problem. Now, brainstorm five creative solutions for this problem. Remember, no idea is too crazy. Just let your creativity flow!

....

....

....

....

....

....

....

....

The Light Bulb Moment: Fostering Innovative Thinking

Every once in a while, you have those light bulb moments when a unique idea pops into your mind out of nowhere. It feels like a burst of electricity sparking your thoughts, illuminating a path you hadn't noticed before. It's as if the entire universe conspires to provide the perfect conditions, the ideal environment for the genesis of innovative thought. But how do we encourage these moments of enlightenment more often?

Firstly, understand that innovative thinking is not exclusive to 'geniuses' or a select few. Anyone, and I mean anyone, can foster creative thinking. And that includes you. The process begins with curiosity which can be a simple question, a spark, or an urge to know more. Embrace this curiosity and ask questions, lots of them. Why is it this way? How does it work? What if we do it differently?

Think of the most recent device you used, your smartphone, perhaps. At some point, someone asked, "What if phones weren't just for making calls? What if they could send messages, take photos, or help us navigate when we're lost?" These questions lead to the multi-purpose devices we have today.

Innovative thinking also involves being open to new experiences. This means stepping out of your comfort zones, exploring different environments, and engaging with diverse cultures and people. These encounters can provide fresh perspectives, which can ignite new ideas.

Finally, remember that innovative thinking requires patience. Not all ideas are born fully formed and ready to change the world. Sometimes, they start as small seeds that need nurturing, watering, and time to grow. It's okay if your ideas don't seem revolutionary at first. Keep refining, learning, and exploring, and who knows, your light bulb moment might just be around the corner.

STAY CURIOUS, BE OPEN, AND HAVE PATIENCE. THE LIGHT BULB IS WAITING TO SHINE ON YOUR BRILLIANT IDEAS.

So, whether you're solving a complex mathematical problem, designing an app, or leading a community project, fostering innovative thinking can be a game-changer. Stay curious, be open, and have patience. The light bulb is waiting to shine on your brilliant ideas.

From Daydreams to Reality: Executing Ideas
Case Study 1: The Green Warriors

In a high school in Texas, a group of friends noticed the food waste produced by their school cafeteria daily. They had an idea to reduce this waste and promote sustainable practices within their school community.

First, they got clarity about their idea—they wanted to implement a composting program and a "share table" where students could leave unopened food for others. They detailed the benefits which mainly included reducing waste and promoting sustainability.

They planned their actions. First, they'd present the idea to the school administration and then organize the logistics. They broke down these steps further: preparing a presentation, setting up meetings, researching composting methods, and designing a system for the share table. The action phase was full of challenges: convincing the school administration, dealing with logistical issues, and educating the student body. But they persevered, adjusting their plan and steadily working through their task list.

Through reflection, they continually improved their systems. They celebrated every successful step: the administration's approval, the first day of the share table, and the first batch of compost.

In the end, they significantly reduced their school's food waste, creating a lasting impact on their community.

Case Study 2: The Tech Titans

In a small town in Indiana, two high school sophomores, Lisa and Jason, shared a passion for technology and coding. They noticed a need for coding education in their school and community and dreamt of creating a coding club.

Firstly, they clearly defined their idea: they wanted to start a coding club that would meet weekly, providing lessons, resources, and collaborative opportunities for young coding enthusiasts. Next, they planned their actions: they needed approval from their school, a meeting space, lesson plans, and a way to publicize the club. They broke these tasks down further, assigning responsibilities and setting deadlines.

The action came next: they prepared their proposal, met with the school principal, designed a curriculum, and advertised the club on social media and flyers. They constantly reflected on their progress and adjusted their plans as they executed their idea. When attendance was lower than expected, they surveyed students to understand the reasons and changed their advertising strategy.

They celebrated each achievement: the principal's approval, the first successful meeting, and each time a club member mastered a new coding skill. Lisa and Jason's coding club not only enhanced their leadership and coding skills but also provided a valuable resource for their community, fostering an environment where more young minds could delve into the captivating realm of coding.

Dreaming and envisioning an idea is just the first step. Bringing that idea to life, transforming it from a mere daydream into a tangible reality, is where the real adventure begins. The transformation from concept to execution is like a potter turning a lump of clay into a beautiful vase; it takes skill, effort, and, most importantly, patience.

So, how do we mould our ideas into reality?

Firstly, get clear about your idea. Just as a blueprint guides a builder, a clear and detailed understanding of your idea will guide your execution process. What exactly is your idea? What is its purpose? Who will benefit from it? The clearer you are about your idea, the smoother your execution process will be.

Next, plan your actions. Break down your idea into smaller, manageable steps or tasks. This approach will render the process more tangible and attainable. Remember, you don't have to construct a skyscraper in a day; initiate by setting a single brick at a time.

Now comes the part where you roll up your sleeves and get your hands dirty. Follow your plan and start ticking off those tasks. Remember, action breeds momentum. The more you act, the closer you get to your goal. And even if you stumble or hit a roadblock, don't let it deter you. Learn from it, adjust your plan if necessary, and keep moving forward.

As you execute your idea, don't forget to pause and reflect. Are things going as planned? What could you do better? Reflection allows you to learn from your actions and make necessary adjustments, keeping you on the right track.

> EVERY TASK COMPLETED, EVERY HURDLE OVERCOME, AND EVERY STEP CLOSER TO YOUR GOAL DESERVES CELEBRATION.

Finally, celebrate your milestones. Every task completed, every hurdle overcome, and every step closer to your goal deserves celebration. It's not solely about crossing the end line but also cherishing the path taken.

 EXERCISE 2:
From Idea to Execution

Choose one of the creative solutions from the first exercise. Now, create a step-by-step plan to implement this idea. What resources will you need? Who can help you? Break down the steps as detailed as possible and set a timeline for each. The goal is to have a practical plan by the end of this exercise.

....

....

....

....

....

....

....

Reflection: After completing these exercises, reflect on the process. Was it challenging to come up with creative solutions? Did you encounter any roadblocks while planning the execution? How did you overcome them? Write down your thoughts and learnings. This reflection will be valuable in your future creative and innovative endeavours.

....
....
....
....
....
....
....
....

Wisdom Wrapping

Turning our daydreams into reality can be a wild ride, full of unexpected twists and turns. It's a journey that tests your resolve, polishes your skills, and ultimately leads you to your destination. So, fasten your seatbelt, hold on firmly, and relish the journey! Your dreams are poised to transform into your reality.

CHAPTER 10

YOUR JOURNEY BEGINS NOW

You've been equipped with the knowledge and tools, been inspired by stories, and gained a better understanding of yourself and the kind of leader you aspire to be. Now, the moment has arrived to put all that knowledge and inspiration to practical use. Leadership isn't a fixed point to reach but rather a continuous path of learning, growth, and transformation. So, strap in, young leaders, for your adventure begins now.

Every marathon starts with the first step, every masterpiece with the first brushstroke, and so does your leadership journey. As John C. Maxwell once said, "The pessimist complains about the wind. The optimist expects it to change. The leader adjusts the sails." This quote beautifully encapsulates the essence of leadership - the ability to adapt and navigate challenges.

You don't have to make monumental changes in your leadership journey overnight. Instead, start with manageable tasks and steadily elevate your objectives. The key is to transition from passive learning to active doing. Take what you have learned and put it into action. It's through taking those initial steps and embracing small changes that you begin to build momentum and develop as a leader.

Remember, leadership is not about waiting for the perfect conditions or expecting circumstances to align in your favour. It's about adjusting your approach and finding solutions when faced with challenges. The quote by Maxwell serves as a reminder that leaders don't complain or passively wait for things to change. They take charge, adapt to the circumstances, and adjust their sails to navigate the winds of change.

Embrace a proactive mindset, adjust your sails when needed, and face challenges with optimism and resilience. By doing so, you will be better equipped to navigate the ever-changing landscape and make a positive impact as a leader.adjusts the sails."

Whether it's taking a stand on an issue you're passionate about, participating in a group project, volunteering for a local charity, or launching an initiative to address a problem in your community, it all begins with a decision to act.

One of the necessary qualities of a leader is having a clear vision. A vision acts like a compass, guiding you through your leadership journey. However, more than knowing where you're going is required. You also need a plan, a map that outlines the route you'll take to reach your destination. The second section of this chapter will show how you can set your leadership goals, chart your course, and measure your progress.

Like any journey, the path to leadership can be fraught with challenges, setbacks, and detours. Sometimes, your energy dips, your spirits flag, and your motivation wane. This is when you need to tap into your power bank—the reservoir of inner strength and inspiration that can fuel your journey. This final segment of this chapter will explore methods that can assist you in maintaining your drive, sustaining your pace, and continuously advancing, regardless of the hurdles you face.

Remember, your leadership journey is unique to you. It's your story to write, a path to carve, and an adventure to live. So, take that first step, embrace the challenges, celebrate the victories, learn from the setbacks, and savour the journey. For the future leader in you, the journey begins now!

The Start Line: From Couch to Action

In the corporate echo chamber of my 18-year career, the unsteady steps of fresh recruits remain etched in my memory. These young minds, poised on the precipice of potential, often stumbled in the twilight between inaction and the commencement of their journey. But with every stumble, they inched closer to the starting line, the threshold of change.

Consider this moment as the beginning of your personal marathon. The couch might seem enticingly comfortable. However, the stories we remember are not those of comfort but of courage. Stories of individuals exchanging the familiar's security for the adventure's uncertainty.

At the starting line of leadership, you lace up your shoes of resolve, wear the helmet of determination, and prepare yourself to make the leap. This first step, as small as it may seem, is monumental. It draws the line between aspiration and action and propels you into a future of limitless possibilities.

Think about an issue in your community which has been causing you worry. Maybe it's an elderly neighbour struggling with grocery shopping or a local park that's become a dumping ground. You've probably thought about ways to address these issues. Maybe you've even discussed them with friends. But how often have you moved beyond conversation to create a solution?

Initiating action is a Herculean task. Doubts might plague your mind, the fear of failure might loom large, and the comfort of inertia might be seductive. These feelings are natural and have been experienced by many leaders at the outset of their journey. The crucial element is to avoid succumbing to these apprehensions.

It's an action that lights the fire of motivation, not the other way around. As you take the first step, the path becomes clearer, and the subsequent steps feel less daunting. With each stride, your confidence will surge, and you'll discover capabilities within yourself that you were oblivious to.

> WITH EACH STRIDE, YOUR CONFIDENCE WILL SURGE, AND YOU'LL DISCOVER CAPABILITIES WITHIN YOURSELF THAT YOU WERE OBLIVIOUS TO.

Picture the issue you've noticed in your community. What if you decided to be the catalyst for change? What if you organized a neighbourhood group to assist the elderly with chores or orchestrated a cleanup drive in the park? This is the starting line. It's time to rise from the couch and set your wheels of change in motion.

In the following sections, we'll delve into strategies for charting your leadership journey and maintaining the spark of motivation. The starting line is under your feet, and your journey awaits. The world is ready to bear witness to your stride. Are you ready to start?

Plotting Your Leadership Quest

In the landscape of leadership, your mission should be clear—a beacon guiding you through the twists and turns of your journey.

However, how can you determine the answer to this question? What is the mission? It's a question that can seem overwhelming, especially when you're just starting out. However, it's less about finding the right answer and more about asking the right questions.

Think back to the problems you identified in the previous chapters. Which of those resonated with you the most? Which issues ignited a spark within you? That spark is often a good indicator of where your mission lies.

Remember, your mission doesn't have to be grand or groundbreaking. Making a positive change in your life can be as simple as adjusting one small habit. It can be helping your school be more environmentally friendly, creating a more inclusive atmosphere in your local community, or helping your peers deal with academic stress.

Once you've identified your mission, it's time to set some goals. These goals will serve as the stepping stones that guide you towards your mission.

Embrace the GROW approach. Make sure your goals are goal-oriented, reality-checked, options-explored, and work-plan-enabled.

Next, draw up a plan. Breaking your goals down into smaller tasks can be a helpful strategy for achieving success. You can avoid feeling overwhelmed and stay motivated if you break down your goals into manageable steps. So, take the time to break your goals down into smaller, achievable tasks and watch yourself make steady progress towards your ultimate goal. Put them in a timeline. This will help you keep track of your progress and adjust your strategy if necessary. Remember to factor in potential challenges and consider how to overcome them.

Plotting your leadership quest is a dynamic process. As you learn and grow, your mission might evolve, your goals might change, and that's okay. Leadership isn't about sticking to a predetermined path; it's about adapting to the terrain, weathering the storms, and always moving forward.

> LEADERSHIP ISN'T ABOUT STICKING TO A PREDETERMINED PATH; IT'S ABOUT ADAPTING TO THE TERRAIN, WEATHERING THE STORMS, AND ALWAYS MOVING FORWARD.

Remember, the real success of this quest isn't in reaching your destination but in the lessons learned, the growth experienced, and the impact made along the way. It's time to plot your course and set sail. Your leadership quest awaits!

The Power Bank: Fueling Your Motivation

Occasionally, there are instances where our levels of energy are depleted, and our productivity is hindered. Feel drained, our goals seem distant, and our enthusiasm wavers. During these times, our motivation, our inner power bank, becomes crucial. But how do we keep this power bank charged, particularly when the going gets tough?

First, you must understand that motivation isn't a constant, unchanging force. It ebbs and flows, much like the tide. Recognising this can help you manage your expectations. It's vital to realise that there will be days that may go differently than planned. Brimming with energy and productivity.

A reliable way to recharge your power bank is to frequently remind yourself of your 'why.' Why did you embark on this leadership quest in the first place? What's the mission propelling you forward? Reflecting on these questions can reignite your motivation and refocus your efforts.

Maintaining a balance between striving for your goals and caring for your well-being is also essential. **You can't run on an empty tank. Regular breaks, a healthy lifestyle, and self-care practices aren't luxuries; they fuel your power bank needs.**

 WORKSHEET: PLOTTING YOUR LEADERSHIP QUEST

1. Self-Reflection

- Please provide a written explanation for why you wish to begin this endeavour. Your leadership journey. This is your 'why.' Whenever you feel your motivation waning, revisit this.

....
....
....
....
....

2. Goal-Setting

- Based on everything you've learned in this book, what are your short-term and long-term leadership goals?
- How will you measure your progress?

....
....
....
....
....
....
....
....
....
....

3. Action Plan

- Please document the necessary steps that must be taken to put your plan into action. Achieve your leadership goals. Start small and gradually build up.
- What potential obstacles might you encounter and how can you overcome them?

....
....
....
....
....
....
....
....

4. Support Network

- List the people who can support you on your leadership journey.
- How can you maintain these relationships and seek help when needed?

5. Self-Care Plan

- Write down activities that help you relax and recharge.
- What are some ways in which you can include these activities in your daily routine?

6. Victory Log

- Keep a log of your victories, no matter how small. Acknowledge and honour your accomplishments and let them inspire you to persevere.

7. Inspiration Board

- Create an inspiration board, physical or digital, with quotes, images, and anything else that inspires and motivates you.

....

....

....

....

Remember, this is not a one-time activity. It's a living document that will grow and evolve with you on your leadership journey. Keep updating it as you learn and grow.

Your journey begins now. It's a quest that will challenge you, transform you, and ultimately reveal the leader within you. This is your time. Stand tall, embrace the journey, and remember that the world needs your unique leadership brand. Let your journey begin!

Wisdom Wrapping

Acknowledging and celebrating even the smallest accomplishments is important as each of the accomplishments brings you closer to achieving your goals. These moments of progress should be recognised and can boost motivation. It's also helpful to surround yourself with positive influences, such as people who inspire and support you on your journey. They can provide the energy to keep you going, even when facing obstacles. Motivation is essential for leadership and keeping your energy levels high will help you continue progressing towards your goals. Remember, what defines a leader is not how fast they move but their ability to persevere and keep moving forward. So, make sure to keep your energy levels charged and keep striving towards your leadership aspirations.

www.ingramcontent.com/pod-product-compliance
Lightning Source LLC
LaVergne TN
LVHW041610070526
838199LV00052B/3073